INTERACTIONAL MORALITY

INTERACTIONAL MORALITY
A Foundation for Moral Discernment in Catholic Pastoral Ministry

Mark L. Poorman, C.S.C.

GEORGETOWN UNIVERSITY PRESS / WASHINGTON, D.C.

Library of Congress Cataloging-in-Publication Data

Poorman, Mark L.
    Interactional morality : a foundation for moral discernment in
Catholic pastoral ministry / Mark L. Poorman.
       p.   cm.
    Includes bibliographical references.
    1. Christian ethics--Catholic authors. 2. Pastoral theology-
-Catholic Church. 3. Catholic Church--Doctrines. 4. Moral
development. 5. Moral education. I. Title. II. Title: Moral
discernment in Catholic pastoral ministry.
BJ1249.P66 1993   253.5--dc20   93-3803
ISBN 0-87840-536-4 (alk. paper)

Georgetown University Press, Washington, D.C. 20057-1079
© 1993 by Georgetown University Press. All rights reserved.
Printed in the United States of America
10 9 8 7 6 5 4 3 2 1
THIS VOLUME IS PRINTED ON ACID-FREE ∞ OFFSET BOOK PAPER

for My Mom and Dad

Contents

Preface

For many of us in Catholic pastoral ministry, assisting others to discern what is truly moral is an art which often eludes systematic description. While we can all agree that good moral discernment requires comprehensive consideration of the issues at stake, we sometimes are at a loss when we try to describe a workable, practical method for such discernment. Nevertheless, those charged with the here-and-now pastoral life of the church must routinely uncover and carefully explore the dimensions of complex moral issues in everyday settings such as hospital chaplaincy, campus ministry, education, and parish life. What constitutes a sound moral discernment process for these issues? How can ministers begin to test the adequacy of their own methods of assisting with moral discernment? What basic, fundamental shape should these pastoral conversations about moral matters take? We must explicate those questions and we must answer them most sensitively, especially in a post-conciliar Catholic church that cherishes the "sanctuary" of the individual conscience and in which simple deference to magisterial authority on moral matters is increasingly called into question.

By using a cross-disciplinary study of the moral psychology of Norma Haan, the philosophy of John Macmurray, and the theological ethics of James Gustafson as backdrop and starting point, I propose a foundation and a method for pastoral moral discernment based on these interactional theories. By studying the moral character of the pastoral conversation itself, I hope to cast new light on the qualities of good discernment as it is co-constructed by the minister and the one seeking help in such diverse areas of concern as bioethics, sexuality, and justice in the workplace. Following my proposal of an interactional foundation for discernment which is historical, multi-dimensional, communal, creative, and centered on Christ, I offer an overview of the practical pastoral implications of such a foundation. My work is mainly aimed at moral theologians, but I do believe that pastoral ministers and those in training for pastoral ministry may also find it useful in their efforts to describe the dynamics of moral discernment from both theoretical and practical standpoints.

My thanks to the many perceptive colleagues and students who have assisted with the book, as well as to the many others who, as practitioners of the art of seeing and knowing what is right and good, minister tirelessly to those seeking help. These, my brothers and sisters in Christ, have taught me much.

M.P.

Acknowledgments

In writing this book, I have come to owe many debts of gratitude to people who have been of help to me and to this project. I am very pleased to name some of them.

In large part, the structure and content of the book appeared in my dissertation at the Graduate Theological Union at Berkeley. From the outset of my studies there, Bill Spohn was a splendid mentor, guide, and friend. His direction of the work at the time, as well as his continuing interest in it, have been invaluable. I am most blessed to have been initiated by Bill in the academic enterprise of Christian ethics. Norma Haan of the Institute of Human Development at the University of California at Berkeley, whose theory of moral psychology forms the cornerstone of my thesis in the book, was a research scholar of enormous originality, creativity, and breadth of interest. In her specific dedication to the theological implications of interactional morality, she was most encouraging and generous to me in the course of my graduate work. I hope that the book does justice to her legacy. Eliane Aerts, a research associate at the Institute who assumed responsibility for my work after Norma's death, supplied valuable and timely critique of the chapters, especially the chapter dealing with the social interactional proposal. I am grateful for Paul Philibert's facility with both moral psychology and religious ethics. He pointed me toward John Macmurray's philosophy, and Paul's kind and early insistence on the clarity of the overall purpose of the book greatly assisted its eventual completion. Deborah Blake, a friend and student at GTU and devotee of Haan's work, was a wonderful conversation partner in probing Haan's implications for Christian ethics.

Many people at Notre Dame have been important to the writing and publishing of the book. Larry Cunningham, Chair of the Theology Department, provided characteristic enthusiasm and encouragement for the project. Michael Buckley first prompted me to revise the original version for publication. Jim Burtchaell, Richard McCormick, and Monk Malloy thoughtfully read drafts and provided comments along the way. Blake Leyerle, John Cavadini, and Todd Whitmore have been first-rate colleagues, who in the midst of the many demands on their own time, have been gracious supporters. Special thanks belong to my associates in the Master of Divinity program, whose work and good spirits have kept me afloat. Bob Krieg, Regina Coll, John Melloh, Sparky Tavis, and Carole Coffin have all provided a wealth of professional, academic, and personal assistance. They are models of collegial friendship.

During the years of writing the book, I was a member of two communities of the Congregation of Holy Cross. At both Holy Cross Center in Berkeley and at Corby Hall at the University of Notre Dame, I have enjoyed the fraternity of my religious brothers. Paul Doyle has been a stillpoint of sanity and holiness throughout my time at Notre Dame.

John Breslin, former director of Georgetown University Press, suggested important editorial changes and the shape of the overall text of the book. John Staczek, his successor and acting director of the Press, kept faithful communication in a transitional time. Patricia Rayner has been accessible and helpful, keeping the whole thing on schedule.

Personal support during research and writing has come from many sources. Tim Scully, Mike Baxter, John Jenkins, Tom Reardon, and Bob Wicke have known me in all of my varied relationships with the manuscript, and they have remained true friends throughout. My sister Jan's immense help with this book has run the gamut from crisis counseling to substantial editing and checks for theological soundness. Her perspective, her theological acumen, and her friendship have enabled its completion. In this and all other endeavors, I have known the deep love of my family, especially my parents, who have been my primary teachers and models of the value of interactional morality. I dedicate the book to Mom and Dad.

INTERACTIONAL MORALITY

1

INTRODUCTION:
Moral Discernment in Catholic Pastoral Ministry—A Practice in Search of a Method

In writing this book, I have sought to develop an ethic and a method for the moral discernment that occurs in pastoral settings such as parishes, medical centers, and campus ministries. The project itself, a systematic study of the interaction between a minister and a person seeking pastoral assistance, draws on both pastoral and moral theology, and has implications for both. During the ministry that preceded my study, I counseled a number of people whose core issues and questions were moral ones. Abortion, contraception, divorce, service in the armed forces, and extramarital sexuality were common fare in the conversations. These interactions were edifying and instructive for me and, I hope, helpful to others. While I drew on both the normative emphases of moral theology and the tenets of caregiving from pastoral theology and training to inform those interactions, there seemed to be an unavoidable ad hoc quality to the conversations and their resolutions. Moreover, my own sense of sound moral theology was radically challenged and improved by those conversations.

As the dimensions of personal stories and dilemmas unfolded, my horizon of what should be considered as part of moral discernment was broadened. I had been under the mistaken impression that the Catholic moral enterprise was primarily concerned with the application of norms and principles to specific situations. Like many Catholics, I had viewed moral discernment as a mathematical procedure with human beings involved. I had absorbed from earlier study the view that a pastoral application of Catholic moral teaching amounts largely to an allowance for a person's failure to live up to those norms and principles, an artful and compassionate "damage control" on the part of the minister, who merely sought the best possible, but not necessarily the most desirable, resolution. Experience suggested, however, that moral discernment proceeds most effectively when the person seeking assistance and the minister consciously attend to the dimensions of human life that emerge from within the interaction itself. In the very act of relating, a comprehensive means for moral discernment comes to our attention. This experience in actual moral discernment reveals a host of categories and concerns that call for pastoral attention.

Of critical importance to moral discernment is a sense of personal history or narrative. When I assist someone with an ethical issue, the matter of concern is clearer after even a cursory exploration of the person's background. Such exploration helps to establish rapport and empathy and affords a practical and theological perspective by which the person and the issue become elements in a larger ongoing story of God's grace. In pastoral conversations about moral concerns, the tendency of the minister and the one seeking help is to focus almost immediately, often too quickly, on the question, dilemma, or crisis at hand. Often the object of immediate concern, especially in Catholic pastoral settings, is moral culpability or a practical strategy for effective resolution, or both. For such pastoral conversations, casuistry based on principles has long been foundational, while personal contextualizing of the issue has been viewed with suspicion.

But history is essential to discernment. In the simple review of a person's development, both the minister and the discerner gain a sense of reverence for the ways in which God has enabled that person to believe and act in the past. Such a sense of development provides a perspective for interpreting the present moment. For example, the moral development of the discerner, his or her capacity for moral reflection and action, the constellation of virtues and vices that are brought to the discernment, and the ways in which moral decisions have been made previously are central historical concerns.

Another dimension that benefits from careful attention in the discernment process is the role of a person's emotions in the issue or question at hand. The training I received in preparation for ministry laid a heavy stress on attending to the emotions, in providing nondirective empathy and support for the one seeking pastoral care. But it was not until I saw the effect of such emotional care that I came to see its real importance. I realize now that creating an environment of trust and empathy yields a more comprehensive discernment because it addresses both the needs and ends of the whole person, the best person, the moral person. An increasing body of moral theory now proposes that sound moral reflection has an integral emotional aspect.[1]

Two considerations are especially important. First, while discernment does have a rational component, and some may even claim that the rational component is the central feature of good moral reflection, to treat moral discernment as a strictly analytical process is to limit its quality and effectiveness. Logic, deduction, and speculation assist the discernment process, but they require a certain dispassionate distance from their object of concern. Moral reflection is not reasoning alone, any more than the moral life is strictly a matter of knowledge or calculation. In concentrating solely on facts, teachings, arguments, validity, cogency, and even careful use of language, one views the human person incompletely and skews the discernment process.

Second, the emotional state of a person can either increase or decrease the adequacy of moral discernment. Certain feelings and emotional conditions assist the process of moral reflection; others serve to block or impede it. For example, a man who is angry or defensive about the seemingly impersonal medical treatment that his dying mother has received will probably not be as willing or able to engage in the process of discerning whether to discontinue her respirator as a woman in the same situation who is confident in the medical protocol offered to her mother and grateful for the gift of her mother's long life.

The most fruitful pastoral conversations in my experience contained a distinct sense that a discerner and I were engaging in a creative process concerning a moral issue or question. Conversations started with some "givens," proceeded within certain parameters, and aimed at a satisfactory closure or resolution, but there was a tenor or quality to the best of those conversations that can only be described as imaginative or resourceful. For a critical portion of the conversation, the dialogue was open-ended. For example, in a case of extramarital sexuality, the pastoral consultation was almost always compelled by an existing relationship that needed definition, evaluation, or direction. Even with the moral critiques of relativism and situationism firmly in my mind, once the interaction began, I often had a clear sense that the interchange could end up in a number of different places. Our discourse was characterized by creativity, subjectivity, induction, and imagination. Such a plurality of possible resolutions has to be seen not as a threat but as a recognition of the freedom and responsibility of the moral agents involved. To resist the temptation to do more talking than listening and more teaching than learning is to take seriously the broad range of goodness and possibility in the human condition. While there remains a certain significance to univocal objective responses to moral quandaries and issues, those responses become starting points rather than ending points in pastoral practice.

The moral discernment that occurred in these sessions was truly dialogic in nature. As I continually examined my role in the process of discernment, I came to view it as more enabling than didactic and authoritative. Along with many other ministers trained in the post-Rogerian age of professionalized pastoral care, I was skeptical about the ultimate value of "active listening" and "counseling in an echo chamber." But the worth of simply sustaining an authentic interaction, of providing cues, of asking open questions, and of suspending judgment, proved itself over time. I did, of course, occasionally instruct or challenge, but only in the context of a wider give-and-take that had already been established. No minister can make the claim that he or she acts strictly as a peer in a counseling session, but I found that when the tenor and conduct of these sessions were genuinely and mutually interactional, people had the license and ability to discern well.

I also found that the interaction itself was an appropriate and helpful expression of the communitarian nature of belonging to a church. Such interactions make the critical point that the moral life of a believer ought to be discerned with the assistance of other believers. Many pastoral theorists project ideals about the central importance of community in moral discernment, but few congregations, parishes, or intentional religious communities actually practice such discernment. The disparity shows itself all too evidently in areas such as worship, education, and social life. As Robert Bellah has aptly shown, the individualism of the North American ethos has successfully eclipsed the various communal promptings of church membership. Nowhere is this eclipse more apparent than in the Christian's moral life. The believer left to his or her own devices negotiates a way through moral challenges by means of private thoughts. One's sense of accountability to a Christian community or, more dramatically, to a Christian tradition has waned. While the idea of the primacy of personal conscience seems to have taken root in the Catholic church,[2] the notion that the conscience should be formed in a communal setting has not. Moral discernment done in a conversation characterized by mutuality and reciprocity, not only achieves a moral balance of perspectives in its resolution, but also effectively teaches both the discerner and the minister that the Christian moral life is communal.

These pastoral conversations about moral issues were occasions to find God and to remember the Spirit of Christ in our midst. They impressed on me the theological truth of the Spirit specifically present in the relationships of Christians. God was present beyond the instances of "God-talk," beyond the discerners' articulated sense of God, relationship to Christ, or interpretations of scripture, though those were essential to the process. I came to see in the course of these encounters, that an interactional model or paradigm for moral discernment, one in which compassion, understanding, and truth are at the core of a genuine conversation, is one that invigorates the moral discernment of believers with a sense of God's immanent presence. One of the primary faults of some Catholic pastoral practice is that moral reflections are largely practical, legal, and prudential in yielding to the immutable moral order of a commanding God. My hope is that an interactional model of discernment for ministers and those seeking assistance will recover an awe and reverence for a loving God of living history who resides in, and is discerned in, the Christian moral life.

Hence the genesis of this book. With this pastoral experience as a backdrop, I explore the possibility of moral theories or perspectives that will support, nuance, and complement these insights. With the help of such theories, I hope to propose systematically a revitalized base and method of doing moral discernment in Catholic pastoral practice. In the book, I attempt to construct a foundational ethic and a critical method for pastoral moral discernment, that is, for the consideration of a personal situation in a Catholic ministerial setting by which a moral course of action is determined. By a "foundational ethic," I mean a system of basic values by which to guide the practice of pastoral moral discernment. By a "critical" method, I mean a method that is informed and shaped by the basic values of this foundational ethic. I think that pastoral ministers, as one of my intended audiences, will appreciate that this work addresses a lacuna in Catholic pastoral practice with regard to moral guidance. Since the decline of the manualist tradition in Catholic moral theology, pastoral guidance has been done in an uneven manner, artful at best, and careless and damaging at worst.

I offer the project in service of Catholic pastoral ministry, which is still laboring over what it means to do pastoral translations of moral teachings. As I explain in the final chapter, Paul VI's encyclical on the regulation of birth, *Humanae Vitae,* exemplifies the existing method of pastoral translation of moral teachings in the Catholic tradition as one that is principally a matter of the minister promulgating and enforcing magisterial teaching, yet allowing compassionate room for those who cannot live up to the ideals of a particular teaching. This compassionate approach, which is actually reducible to the forgiveness of sins and the limiting of moral culpability through a plea bargaining of sorts, has served as the pastoral approach to moral problems. In the theoretical arena, this approach has also served as the fundamental scheme for differentiating pastoral and moral theology.[3] In the most difficult moral matters, both Catholic ministers and moral theologians traditionally have employed the distinction between "pastoral" and "moral" as a way of keeping intact challenging and controversial moral teachings while attempting to address the individual needs of believers. For practical reasons, the distinction may be helpful, but it has contributed to a perceived monolithic quality to official teachings. Use of such a distinction has subtly implied that a pastoral resolution of a moral concern is somehow a deficient resolution. But when someone is in the thicket of moral confusion, whether about divorce and remarriage or about an extramarital sexual relationship or about a decision at the boundaries of life, he or she believes that a comprehensive moral discernment yields an answer that can truly balance the many claims on moral life. In the past, a believer's discernment was moral only if it ended in a resolution that was congruent with official teaching. If the resolution was off-center from the teaching because of particular circumstances in the life of the believer, it was tolerated as a pastoral answer.

As a minister convinced of the value of conversation, dialogue, and exchange between persons as means of determining not merely second-rate compromises but real courses of moral action, I have sought to explore in this book the moral meaning of interaction with a view toward establishing a renewed Catholic pastoral moral discernment. Is the conversation between a pastoral minister and a moral discerner primarily an occasion for consolation, empathy, and practical strategizing? Is the balanced outcome of such a conversation moral in nature or merely pastoral? Is not the interaction between persons who are engaged by a moral issue already a moral act in and of itself? If there are truly moral dimensions to the process and outcomes of these pastoral dialogues, what are they, and how might we promote them? The principal thrust of this work is to develop a foundation and a method for a pastoral discernment that is appropriately termed "moral." I provide both methodological underpinnings for such pastoral moral discernment and practical implications for effectively implementing it.

To gain theoretical support for the core value of interaction in moral discernment, I have been attracted to the recent and original studies of Norma Haan and her associates at the Institute of Human Development at the University of California at Berkeley. Haan, who studied moral development with Lawrence Kohlberg prior to her arrival at Berkeley, departed from Kohlberg's theory in a fundamental way. Rather than view moral development as Piaget and Kohlberg do—that is, as the increasing adequacy of cognitive structures—Haan envisions moral development as the acquiring and enacting of social skills, and she sets out to study the ways in which people interact about moral matters.

She has demonstrated that skills of social interaction are highly dependable gauges of moral action and decision making, and that certain interactions prompt better resolutions of moral discussions than others. As I worked with her and her associate, Eliane Aerts, I came to know the implications that interactional morality can have for the theoretical underpinnings of pastoral encounters. Haan has the research designs and empirical data to bear out my hypotheses about interaction and moral discernment. In her studies of young adults and four-year-olds, she made critical discoveries about communication with others in moral matters. Her important work in moral psychology forms the centerpiece of my reformulation of pastoral and moral theology.

While I believe that such an interdisciplinary endeavor is essential to the renewal of Catholic moral theology and pastoral practice, I also think it important to examine the prior question of the admissibility of the empirical science of psychology as a source of ethics, as a moral ground on which to build a foundational ethic and critical method for Catholic pastoral moral discernment. Therefore, in Chapter Two, I offer a brief methodological note by demonstrating a warrant for admitting psychology as a source for moral reflection in the Catholic tradition. In Chapter Three, I provide an extensive review and critique of Haan's valuable contribution in relation to my thesis.

Haan arrived at her interactional theory of morality through the empirical study of psychology. Two other interactional moralists, John Macmurray and James G. Gustafson, came to similar conclusions through moral philosophy and theology, respectively. Although Haan's empirical theories provide a novel, welcome, and deliberate point of departure for this project, her conclusions, which she has characterized as "thin assumptions of value," are effectively complemented by the contributions of Macmurray and Gustafson, who maintain an interactional perspective and accept God and Christian faith in God as centers of value. In Chapter Four, I discuss selected works of Macmurray and Gustafson thematically, again seeking the implications of each for pastoral moral discernment.

After explaining in some detail the elements of the moral life as viewed by these interactional theorists, in Chapter Five I construct from a conversation among them the foundational ethic that reflects the pastoral experience I have outlined. That foundational ethic is historical in its method; multidimensional in its moral anthropology; imaginative and creative in its resolutions toward a course for action; social, relational, and communal in its perspectival approach; and centered on the believer's relationship to God in Christ. In the final chapter, I refer to these features of the proposed foundational ethic in order to draw practical implications for a critically informed method of pastoral moral discernment in the Catholic tradition. I also demonstrate its effect by contrasting it with the pastoral approach prescribed in *Humanae Vitae*. With that, the intended "limited" project of addressing a need for a guiding ethic and a critical method of moral discernment in Catholic pastoral practice is concluded.

In addition to my main purpose of developing a foundational ethic and critical method for pastoral moral discernment, I hope to suggest as a secondary but important theme that the lack of an adequate method of moral discernment in Catholic pastoral settings is a reflection of the much broader conceptual and methodological problem of the distinction between pastoral and moral concerns in Catholic theology. This general distinction is apparent in traditional and contemporary Roman Catholic moral theology and helped to bring me to this specific project.

In the Roman Catholic tradition, disciplinary custom holds that moral theology concerns itself with theological and nontheological principles, values, teachings, and objective standards for the moral life. In that same tradition, pastoral theology concerns itself with the actual, particular, and individual lives and circumstances of believers. The overlap of the two promises to be helpful, and yet that common ground has rarely been mined as a source for theological reflection and renewal for either discipline. In the course of my studies, I discovered that the promptings of pastoral care seem to count for little in moral theology, which is governed by its own internal methods of determining sound argument and theory. Likewise, pastoral theologians, freshly renewed by rapprochement with therapeutic tenets of nonjudgmentalism, are skeptical of the value of a dialogue with moral theologians, who they believe are more interested in moralizing.

I have contented myself with studying and writing about moral theology from a pastoral point of view, attempting to interject some sense of practicality in the convolutions of moral theory and looking to entertain discussions of values and standards in the art of pastoral care. But the separation of the two continues. The distinction between pastoral and moral theology may be witnessed not only in Roman Catholic magisterial moral theology, but in the work of many moral theologians serving the Catholic tradition. I have based this book on interactional theorists, hoping to open moral discernment to the evaluative categories that may be discovered in pastoral encounters. These categories include character, emotions, senses and intuitions, imagination, intellect, relationships, moral development, situation, perception, and communal wisdom. In part, these efforts were generated by my interest in the traditional hard distinction between moral theology based on a statically conceived, objective, natural law and pastoral theology based on individual experience, situation, and belief. One of the first to acknowledge this fundamental difficulty and the hint of an impending paradigm shift for moral theology was Eric Doyle, who stated the following in response to an ongoing debate about the basic thrusts of moral and pastoral theology:

> The most serious difficulties for an exclusively nature-based moral theology, which is concerned primarily to establish abstract, detailed, immutable and universally applicable norms, arise from the open conflict between most of the principles of this moral theology and the findings of the behavioral sciences, the pastoral experience of priests, Christian counsellors and social workers and the daily experience of a rapidly increasing number

of believers in the Church. The conflict is caused chiefly because
the principles of this nature-based morality deal with "ideal," not
with real people, with "ideal" not with real situations, and because it offers no help whatever in the concrete circumstances of
life in the Church and the world.[4]

In his recent masterful history of Roman Catholic moral theology,
John Mahoney makes a similar observation about the revered but relatively unexamined distinction between pastoral decision and moral
science, which has many implications for both moral theology and
pastoral practice. His words are worthy of quoting at length:

> The reluctance of moral theology, as it has developed, to incor-
> porate the particular, and the relinquishing of the individual to
> "pastoral" theology and to "pastoral" solutions to moral dilem-
> mas (which has also until recently prevented any healthy de-
> velopment of pastoral theology), may arise partly from a desire
> to preserve the character of moral theology as a theological sci-
> ence, and from a care to maintain its self-esteem as a "hard"
> rather than a "soft" science in the face of moral philosophy or eth-
> ics. And yet, as a branch of theology, the description of moral the-
> ology as a "science" is but an analogy which is ill-used if its
> comparison with purely human counterparts is pushed too liter-
> ally and univocally.[5]

Mahoney goes on to evaluate the recent efforts in Catholic moral theology to account for the particularities of pastoral situations:

> It is interesting to note, however, how, alongside major new
> developments in pastoral theology, much recent work in moral
> theology has been at pains to explore avenues which integrate the
> particular into the renewal of the subject, largely stimulated by
> the reflection on so-called "conflict" situations. Theories of choos-
> ing the lesser of two evils, or more positively of choosing the best
> in the circumstances, of compromise, of proportionality, of situ-
> ated or limited freedom, and others, appear to be so many
> acknowledgements that moral theology cannot today simply con-
> tent itself with elaborating a list of moral universals without also
> carefully perusing their absolute or relative character, notably
> when they may, or may "appear," to come into conflict in partic-
> ular situations or for particular individuals.[6]

A significant renewal of moral theology may occur by relating moral
theology to the demands of pastoral situations. Mahoney's crowning
insight describes this critical juncture in the history of moral theology:

It may appear, then, that various current attempts to incorporate particulars into the science of moral theology, with all the mental and systematic adjustments which that implies, is a move to throw a bridge across the gap between "objective" and "subjective" morality and to judge that, far more frequently than has been suspected, what diverse individuals consider God requires of them is in actual fact what God does "objectively" require of them, as legitimate personal diversities.[7]

In the light of Doyle's and Mahoney's evaluations of Catholic moral theology, and in keeping with my own nascent convictions that some of the best moral theology is forged in the balance of "pastoral solutions," I modestly submit that this book will fill a pastoral need by supplying a theory and method for Catholic moral discernment. In its examination of the moral dimensions of pastoral relationships and dialogues, it may also contribute to a renewed Catholic moral theology based on the actual lives of Christian believers.

NOTES

1. See, for example, Sidney Callahan, *In Good Conscience* (New York: Harper Collins, 1991) and William C. Spohn, S.J., "Passions and Principles," in Notes on Moral Theology: 1991, *Theological Studies* Volume 52 (March 1990): 69–87.

2. An excellent empirical treatment of this theme may be found in Patrick H. McNamara, *Conscience First, Tradition Second* (Albany, NY: State University of New York Press, 1992).

3. For a concise discussion of this distinction in Roman Catholic moral theology, see Richard Gula, *Reason Informed By Faith: Foundations of Catholic Morality* (New York: Paulist Press, 1989), 306–308. See also Charles E. Curran, "The Pastoral Minister, the Moral Demands of Discipleship and the Conscience of the Believer" in *Directions in Fundamental Moral Theology* (Notre Dame: University of Notre Dame Press, 1985), see pp. 257–280.

4. Eric Doyle, O.F.M., "Peaceful Reflections on the Renewal of Moral Theology," *The Clergy Review* 62 (October 1977): 393–401.

5. John Mahoney, *The Making of Moral Theology: A Study of the Roman Catholic Tradition* (Oxford: Clarendon Press, 1989), 329.

6. Ibid.

7. Ibid., 330.

2

A NOTE ON METHOD:
Warrants for Using Experience, Empirical Science, and Psychology

Established sources for Christian moral reflection include philosophy, religious tradition, sacred scripture, and the experience of the believer. In Roman Catholic moral theology and especially in the official teaching of the Catholic magisterium, philosophy and tradition have been the principal sources in developing a method for ethics. Among Catholic moral theologians and to some extent the magisterium, this basic methodological stance has begun to change in the past thirty years. Increasingly, both sacred scripture and the collective and individual experience of believers are enjoying some acceptance as important sources for determining areas of discernment and courses of action in the Christian moral life.

This historical development is itself worthy of a detailed study that cannot be attempted here. Briefly, there has been an incremental but certain realization that Roman Catholic ethics based strictly on natural law philosophy and teachings promulgated by previous popes, bishops, and magisteria has been found wanting in two areas. First, the role of Christian faith seemed to be minimized in a system of ethics that stresses the "natural." Second, the applicability of Catholic ethical thought based on a classical worldview and past Church teaching has waned in the face of contemporary situations that demand more comprehensive ethical considerations.

In answer to the first deficiency, Catholics have begun to appreciate and incorporate the writings of Christian ethicists whose main focus is the role of scripture in the moral life. Examples abound, including Karl Barth's encounter of the commands of God in scripture, H. Richard Niebuhr's interpretation of events through the lens of scripture, Gustavo Gutierrez's focus on the liberation themes of scripture, and Stanley Hauerwas's careful articulation of the formation and transformation of character through the narrative accounts of scripture.[1] While some Catholics have begun simply to appropriate these methods as alternatives to former sources, others such as Josef Fuchs and Bernard Häring have attempted a methodological dialogue between scripture and a traditional Catholic source, natural law.[2] This incorporation of scripture into Catholic ethical reflection began in scholarly circles prior to Vatican II and was then encouraged by the council itself.[3] It has provided a necessary and welcome shift in method which has both deepened and broadened the consideration of morality.

Response to the second deficiency, the waning effectiveness of church teaching in the face of complex contemporary situations, has been slow and uneven. Less influential than the role of scripture has been the role of experience and its systematic consideration in the empirical sciences. Although generations of Catholic moral theologians in the manualist tradition seemed to suggest by their casuistry prepared for confessors that concreteness in the assessment of the moral life was important, experience as such was suspect as a locus for method. Ethical method in the manualist tradition really amounted to an intricate application of a deductive, syllogistic procedure that exhibited deep distrust for working inductively from experience to teaching. Because the development of the empirical sciences was a late phenomenon relative to the tenure of the manualist tradition, and perhaps because of a continuing distrust of the data of experience, it is not surprising there is no evidence of a strictly empirical consideration of the human condition by the manualists.

Catholic moral anthropology, derived from natural law and articulated by the manualist tradition, did not seek the assistance of either the hard sciences, such as biology or chemistry, or the social sciences, such as psychology or sociology. As a result, the effectiveness of moral reflection in the Catholic tradition was impoverished, both in its theoretical aspects, such as the formulation of official teaching, and in its practical aspect, pastoral moral discernment. But experience and empirical science, like sacred scripture, are slowly finding their place as admissible sources for Catholic moral reflection.

In this chapter, I will set the methodological stage for the discussion of a specific psychological theory of morality in the next chapter.

Prior to reviewing and examining the social interactional theory of morality proposed by Norma Haan, which will serve as a theoretical cornerstone for this project, I will address two fundamental questions: How can we presume to use human experience and its articulation in an empirical science to determine the shape and content of Catholic moral reflection, and, more specifically, where in the Catholic tradition does one find warrants for using a psychological theory of morality to propose an ethic and method for Catholic pastoral moral discernment? To answer these questions, I will examine two foundational Catholic sources for ethical method, natural law and the official teaching tradition of the church as articulated by various bodies including popes, bishops, and sacred congregations. The task at hand is to search these widely authorized Catholic sources for internal justifications for the use of psychology in determining both the shape and the content of moral reflection.

I. Natural Law, Experience, and the Use of Empirical Science in Moral Reflection

The natural law perspective has been a consistent cornerstone of Catholic moral thought, and it would seem a particularly apt place to seek a justification for the introduction of a source that may as yet be outside the principal stream of Catholic ethics. The general acceptance of the natural law tradition in Catholic circles, in the theological and magisterial communities, prompts us to look to it as a legitimating force for our purposes. As Charles Curran has noted,

> It must always be recalled that there is general agreement within the Roman Catholic tradition that the human plays a large role in Christian morality. . . . The moral theology of the manuals . . . gave great importance to the role of the human in Christian ethics, . . . the teaching of the hierarchical magisterium on social matters was explained almost exclusively in terms of the natural law which is common to all mankind. In addition, those teachings which can be looked upon as most distinctively Catholic, such as the condemnation of contraception, sterilization, abortion, euthanasia, as well as the principle of the double effect, have all been based on natural law. . . .[4]

There is also a less conservative reason for attending to the natural law. It is a tradition worthy of our regard because it offers sound insights into the sources and shape of the moral life. First, it tells us that we may look to our common human living as a source for determining how we should live. Second, according to Catholic tradition, the use of human reason in such a determination is trustworthy. Third, when we wish to learn or teach about such human strivings, a natural law perspective will allow us to direct our attention not only to our own narrow circumstances but to a wider human audience.

But this perspective that is commonly called natural law is not an easy one to locate and characterize. It has endured a number of theoretical mutations through the centuries, and despite its wide acceptance in Catholic thought as a basis for method, much needs to be settled in regard to its actual constitution. In fact, according to a certain previous understanding of natural law within the church, empirical science would have been excluded from the purview of ethical reflection.

The fundamental contention of natural law is that we may know what we should do by attending to human nature. It would seem that empirical science, a systematic consideration of human life and experience, would be a fitting partner in attending to that nature. Curran summarizes the relationship:

> The coalition of Catholic theology with rational Greek philosophy shows the openness of such theology to the insights of reason and the sciences. A theology which is open to insights of reason is thus in principle open to the data of science. . . . The judgments of reason do depend upon sense data as a starting point so that empirical data should enter into the final intellectual judgment about the order implanted by God in the universe.[5]

The emphasis in the natural law perspective on reason and experience is the perfect window for the admission of empirical science. But this reflects a broader view of natural law. It is unfortunate that certain philosophical and theological interpretations of natural law have narrowed the notion, especially in Catholic tradition. More recently, there have been attempts to recover its rich dimensions in revised notions of natural law. In order to fully appreciate the tradition as a whole, its attendant historical difficulties, and the contributions of its revisions, we now turn to a discussion of the evolution of natural law within the Catholic tradition, paying particular attention to it as an allowable base on which rests empirical science as a methodological source.

Greco-Roman Origins

Natural law can be traced to classical Greek culture, which gave it one of its eminent characteristics, the description of the human condition in ideal form. The Greeks conceived of the manifold differences among human beings as merely accidental ones that were exceptions to the ideal state of humanity. Humanity in turn was part of an overall reality that was ordered, complete, and unchanging.

Given these two contentions, the basic premise of natural law was that human beings in their many expressions ought to live according to a single ideal form predicated on an unchanging reality. Failure to align oneself with this ideal form and its underlying reality resulted in tragedy, well documented, for example, in Greek drama. Human will and intention predictably played volatile roles in this conception. When such intentions were in league with the givenness of reality, order prevailed and happiness ensued. When one sought to order life differently than it had been divinely ordained, one suffered the consequences. Douglas Sturm outlines the features of this Greek mind-set that are central to the development of the natural law tradition and particularly germane to our eventual discussion of the Christian appropriation of the tradition.

First, according to Sturm, this was an organic rather than a mechanistic mind-set. That is, all things fit together into a living whole and each part derives its entire definition from the fact that it is a part of a greater reality, not a thing unto itself. Consequently, all things in the universe possess innate tendencies governed by the larger, well-ordered reality. Second, this mind-set took as its point of departure the human rather than the divine as is witnessed by the Greeks' anthropocentric obsession in their poetry, sculpture and painting, and their gods.[6] In short, according to Sturm, "it is an understanding of reality that is naturalistic, humanistic, immanentalistic and nonhistorical."[7] Moreover, as Timothy O'Connell has pointed out in this conception, human participation in the universe is largely passive, with the particular moral challenge being the "obligation (perceived by reason) to conform to nature."[8]

Roman influence on the development of the natural law tradition is divided into two major movements. The general tendency in the Roman influence was toward the "law" aspect of natural law. The Romans, unlike the Greeks, were not completely wedded to the notion that conformity to a static cosmos constituted one's moral obligation. Instead, Romans celebrated human activity, reason, and creativity as sources for moral determinations, thus stressing the reasonable as the distinctively human. Reason itself was natural, and its exercise was the necessary agreement with nature that was mandated by "natural law." In Timothy O'Connell's assessment of Roman natural law, "what [was] natural [was] right reason, human intelligence, prudent and thoughtful action directed to humane ends. Here [was] no abject capitulation to the facts of life."[9]

Indeed, we find this active notion of natural law in Cicero and Gaius, who gave us *jus civile*, the law of the particular society or collective, and *jus gentium*, the more generic law that governs all peoples. The major exception to this basic Roman perspective was Ulpian's *jus naturale*, a natural law more akin to the Greek notion of natural law. Ulpian described the natural law as a "rule of action common to man and all the animals." By introducing animals into the picture, Ulpian effectively described humanity as one among many species that is subject, like the animals, to rules of the natural world. Gone was the notion of the distinctiveness of humanity based on the right exercise of reason and prudence. Instead, as O'Connell concludes, Ulpian and those influenced by him "saw the natural law as the demand placed upon human beings to be what they are, to conform themselves to the facts of life, to accept themselves and their fate, to be docile fellow-animals in the world."[10] Ulpian's contribution to natural law theory becomes critical as we later examine his influence on various medieval sources, including Thomas Aquinas. Specifically, we will be interested in two major implications of Ulpian's amendment of the Roman tradition with a return to Greek categories. First, as "nature" becomes that which we share with the animals rather than our use of reason, basic moral anthropology develops a two-tiered understanding of "human." Curran describes the theoretical snag:

> A top layer of rationality is merely added to an already constituted bottom layer of animality. The union between the two layers is merely extrinsic—the one lies on top of the other.[11]

The extrinsic quality of reason in turn accentuates the definition of "animality," such that the various features of animality, or simple biological processes, become major criteria for what is natural:

> The animal layer retains its own finalities and tendencies, independent of the demands of rationality. Thus the individual may

not interfere in the animal processes and finalities. . . . Ulpian's notion of nature easily leads to a morality based on the finality of a faculty independent of any considerations of the total human person or the total human community.[12]

As we shall see later, the "finalities" and "tendencies" in animal life become critical points of reference as others develop these into physical "faculties" from which we draw our cues about the moral life. Augustine, for example, capitalized on the two-tiered notion of nature, stressing the necessity to be aware of the division in humanity between the lower dictates of animality and the higher promptings of human reason. He mediates the two through his well-known concept of "right ordering" of the things of the universe:

> When reason controls the movement of the soul, man is said to be ordered. For it is not a right order or even to be called order at all, when the better is subject to the worse.[13]

Or, as Mahoney summarizes the principal contribution of Augustine in this regard, a contribution that will have lasting impact on Catholic appropriation of natural law theory in moral theology,

> all the things which God has created are good, and so the rational soul acts well with reference to them if it maintains order, and if by distinguishing, choosing, and assessing, it subordinates the lesser things to the greater, the bodily to the spiritual, the lower to the higher and the temporal to the eternal.[14]

Thomas Aquinas

Accurate portrayal of Thomas Aquinas's notion of natural law has become increasingly important, especially as we consider the later influence of the manualist tradition, which claimed Thomas as its primary architect. An adequate treatment of his theory of natural law cannot be presented here.[15] Suffice it to say for our present purposes that what is at stake in investigating Thomas's conception of natural law is whether he would admit the typically Roman role of reason or whether he sought to portray the natural law in the Greek terms of a completed universe to which we must conform. Whereas the former would more readily admit the value of personal experience in moral discernment (and, by extrapolation, its systematic formulation in empirical science), the latter, with its static worldview and all the precepts humans need to know, would be less amenable to them as credible sources.

O'Connell and Curran note that Thomas's writings reveal a grounding in both the order of nature and the order of reason.[16] In Parts I–II, Question 94, Article 2, we find, in adjacent passages, the following explanations of the constitution of natural law:

> There is in man an inclination to things that pertain to him more specially, according to that nature which he has in common with other animals: and in virtue of this inclination, those things are said to belong to the natural law, which nature has taught to all animals, such as sexual intercourse, education of offspring and so forth.[17]

Thomas adds as his next point:

> There is in man an inclination to good, according to the nature of his reason, which nature is proper to him: thus man has a natural inclination to know the truth about God and to live in society: and in this respect, whatever pertains to this inclination belongs to the natural law.[18]

Other observations are worthy of note in this discussion of the Thomistic formulation of natural law. Although evidence may be readily supplied to demonstrate Thomas's ambivalence about the ascendancy of the "order of reason" or the "order of nature," we get several glimpses of the Thomistic formulation as one which is at least quite accommodating to the order of reason.

First, Thomas's use of Aristotle suggests an approval of the order of reason. I will prescind for now from the fact that Aristotle was for Thomas a contemporary source (thus already suggesting an openness to the development of thought that runs counter to the ahistorical quality of the classical order of nature).[19] Still, the order of reason seems to receive structural support from Aristotelian thought as a foundation for natural law. Human life is not most keenly described by comparison with the faculties of animals, but by attending to the special qualities allowed by reason.

Second, Thomas had a refined notion of the role of prudence in the moral life. The centrality of this virtue again suggests the prominence of reason and, more important, that living the moral life requires a rigorous discernment, not merely an assent to the prompt-ings of preprogrammed faculties:

> Now man is suitably directed to his due end by a virtue which perfects the soul in the appetitive part, the object of which is the good and the end. And to that which is suitably ordained to the due end, man needs to be rightly disposed by a habit in his reason, because counsel and choice, which are about things ordained to the end, are acts of the reason. Consequently, an intellectual virtue is needed in the reason, to perfect the reason, and make it suitably affected towards things ordained to the end; and this virtue is prudence. Consequently, prudence is necessary to lead a good life.[20]

Finally, and germane to our discussion about the role of experi-ence and empirical science in moral discernment, Thomas allowed adequate room for arriving at different conclusions to moral dilem-mas. Based on his contention that as one proceeds from the primary principles of natural law to more specific ones, he notes that as one approaches the concrete situation at hand, numerous courses of action emerge as possible:

> Consequently we must say that the natural law, as to general principles, is the same for all, both as to rectitude and as to knowledge. But as to certain matters of detail, which are conclu-sions, as it were, of those general principles, it is the same for all in the majority of cases, both as rectitude and as to knowledge; and yet in some few cases it may fail . . .[21]

Such modesty in claims about the comprehensiveness of the nat-ural law in serving all aspects of the moral life seems to imply an admission of latitude of conclusions in moral discernment which, as we shall see, was ignored by the manualists. But more important for our present purposes, right reason and the prudential assessment of particular situations are integral to Thomas's theory of natural law. Experience and its articulation would seem welcome partners in such a notion of "natural."

The Manualist Tradition

The unity and coherence of Thomas's moral theology was mini-mized and even abandoned by succeeding commentators and theorists.[22] Of special significance were the followers of William of Ockham and the movement of Nominalism, who have been cited as the source of a new fragmentation in moral theology. According to Bernard Häring's assessment:

> The Ockhamists were responsible for the fateful decline in moral theology. At the fountainhead of the development of the moral theology of the fourteenth century is the baneful metaphysics of William of Ockham. The fundamental intuition of nominalism is the unique value of the singular, the individual. The only true reality is the individual. Only the particular man, the human individual, really exists.[23]

The Ockhamists clearly employed metaphysical foundations to underplay or abandon Thomas's sound intuitions about habits informed by reason in favor of an analysis of individual acts driven by will. On the heels of the influence of the Ockhamists, the publication of penitential books, manuals designed for the use of a confessor in advising penitents about particular acts, flourished.[24]

A Thomistic revival in the sixteenth century provided some antidote to the increasingly act-oriented considerations of moral theology, but the unified features of Thomas's theology were not recovered. Instead, a lasting split occurred between the speculative quality of Thomas's systematic theology and the commentaries on his moral theology. Although a number of different commentaries on the *Summa Theologica* were born during this period, several historical events allowed for the prominence of those stressing practicality. Notable among such historical events were the Counter-Reformation with its concern about justification and free will (with a concomitant preoccupation with acts), and the rise in importance of the sacrament of penance according to the Council of Trent.[25]

The preparation of confessors was the goal of these later manuals, which were more comprehensive than earlier penitential manuals had been, but still very much engaged by the practical problems of settling the penitent's conscience. As a further means of providing explicit answers to questions of conscience, canon law was later assimilated by the manuals. During the seventeenth and eighteenth centuries, moral theology continued in the vein of manuals, laws, and cases of conscience, and came to be viewed as a separate enterprise from systematic and dogmatic theology. In an effort to hone the abilities of theologians and confessors, seminary training developed methods for adjudicating "doubtful" consciences.

The manualist tradition continued in the nineteenth and twentieth centuries, weathering a conflict between German and Italian moral theologians (settled by Pius IX's intervention in *A Syllabus of Errors*). Toward the mid-twentieth century, some attempts to accentuate a more integrated approach to the moral life surfaced through the inclusion of scripture and patristics.[26] As no substantive changes in the preparation of confessional ministry occurred, however, the legal paradigm endured through the 1950s. Priests and seminarians continued to study such classics as Heribert Jone and Dominic Prummer as the keys to moral theology.

How, then, might we evaluate this interpretation of the natural law tradition by the manualists and its neo-scholastic revival in the nineteenth and twentieth centuries? Generally speaking, this interpretation of the natural law tradition has been the most enduring and pervasive one in the Catholic tradition. The Counter-Reformation translation of Thomistic natural law has served as the core of moral theology for four centuries, and its influence on Catholic thought and life cannot be underestimated. In our efforts to admit experience and empirical science into the currency of Catholic moral reflection, the manualist tradition of natural law presents the most resistance.

Perhaps the most salient feature of the manualist notion of natural law morality is its election of a classical rather than a historical worldview.[27] Lonergan describes these worldviews—the classicist and historicist—as two "apprehensions" of the person, as moral anthropologies that adequately summarize a host of theological foundations for the consideration of human nature. The classical worldview emphasizes the conservative, the traditional, and the abstract; and is generally concerned with properties verifiable in every person. "Human" and "natural" are unchanging abstractions. In this worldview, there is little room for changing forms, structures, or methods because all change is in the concrete, and in this view the concrete is always omitted. (As we will note later, Lonergan does not consider this worldview as congenial to a theological understanding of humanity, precisely because it does not consider the concrete circumstances of life. Accordingly, God seems to be active only in structures and forms, but not in events.)

A historical worldview emphasizes the modern and the liberal, as ratified in the repudiation of old models and methods, and focuses on the exercise of freedom, creativity, and initiative. I quote at length

Lonergan's key insight about the importance of the historical quality of human life:

> a concrete aggregate developing over time where the locus of development and, so to speak, the synthetic bond of emergence, expansion, differentiation, dialectic of meaning and meaningful performance. On this view intentionality, meaning, is a constitutive component of human living; moreover, this component is not fixed, static, immutable, but shifting, developing, going astray, capable of redemption; on this view, there is in historicity, which results from human nature, an exigency for changing forms, structures, methods; and it is on this level and through this medium of changing meaning that divine revelation has entered the world and that the Church's witness is given to it.[28]

In its articulation of what is "natural," the manualist tradition was first and foremost classicist in its moral anthropology. It was in large part a closed, monolithic system that proceeded from timeless principles about human life and embraced a deductive, a priori method.[29] The historical worldview, on the other hand, in attending to the particular and the concrete, is inductive and a posteriori in its method. The historical understanding quite clearly allows for experience as a critical source for moral reflection; the classicist does not.[30]

A second feature of the manualist conception of natural law is that it placed natural law at the virtual center of an overarching legal paradigm for the moral life. Although the starting point of the manuals of moral theology was the end of humanity—life with God—the means to that end, laid out in remarkable detail, was submission to laws of every kind. One representative work, for example, was the *Handbook of Moral Theology*, by Dominic Prummer, O.P. In its introductory treatises, "human acts" merit nineteen pages of coverage, "conscience," nine pages, "virtues in general," two pages, and "law," thirty-one pages. In this well-known conception, natural law was "the rational creature's participation in the eternal law," which was "the divine reason or will commanding the preservation of the natural law and forbidding its disturbance."[31] This conception of natural law gave rise to the notions of divine and natural law, from which came the more explicit secondary precepts of the human law.[32] The eventual conflation of moral theology and canon law only added strength to this exaggerated legal paradigm which used natural law as its centerpiece.

The third noteworthy feature of the manualist notion of natural law, consistent with the elaborate legal paradigm, is that individual human acts took on undue importance as indicators of compliance or noncompliance with natural law and, subsequently, with Catholic morality. The obsession with violation, ignorance, intention, penalties, and censures, for example, reveals an act-mentality which may be rooted in either the Ockhamist development or the earlier influence of Ulpian on Thomas. Fascination with the physical structure of the act as the indicator of moral wrongness led to another feature of the manualist purchase on natural law, namely, a disposition to "biologism" and "physicalism." Indeed, this disposition has endured in official statements of church moral teaching even to present times.[33]

Finally, as one may infer from the above features of the manualist tradition, Thomas Aquinas was used selectively as a foundation for later developments of this system. Absent, for example, is Thomas's ambivalence about the order of reason. Moreover, the order of nature seems to have disappeared in the manualist conception of natural law. The Greeks' (and Ulpian's) propensity for the order of nature and their influence on Thomas seem to have resulted in a diminution of the role of reason.

Revisions of the Natural Law Tradition and the Roles of Experience and Empirical Science

I turn now to theoretical movements within philosophy and theology that prize natural law insights about morality but also offer some revisions as "friendly amendments." These amendments stand to revitalize the tradition in general and are particularly amenable to the admission of experience and empirical data in morality. As we shall see, most of the revisions are directed toward the manualist conception of natural law.

One major concern is the ahistorical quality of the natural law system as it has been promulgated in the Greek/Ulpian/manualist strain. This criticism takes many forms, but one principal theological insight, perhaps best articulated by Karl Rahner, is sufficient for our purposes. According to Rahner, any notion of an immutable human nature runs directly counter to Christian faith and theology, which are rooted in a historical phenomenon—the life, ministry, death, and resurrection of Jesus Christ. This revelation, and theological reflection on it, are both historical expressions, and the Christian is immersed in a real, concrete, and continuous salvation history—not merely as an object of fate but as a subject who participates in that history.[34] Still no hopeless divorce exists between the natural law and Christian traditions. Quite to the contrary, as Sturm points out, a foundational connection links the historical approach of Christianity and the classicist approach of natural law:

> Christ is the restoration of the true image of man, because he is the incarnation of the love which is the meaning of our existence. . . . With the coming of Christ. . . . is an effective disclosure in action of what the attitude and purpose and character of God always was, always is and always will be. Thus the God of our redemption is the same as the God of our creation.[35]

The admission of a historical dynamism into the natural law perspective is perhaps the most important and comprehensive revision of all. It carries with it several other implications. First, the admission of historicity into the natural law perspective allows that one may turn less to the cosmos and more to the person for the basis of moral reflection. That is, if the human person is not merely a pawn of predetermined nature but an agent of change and a participant in human history, as Rahner would have it, then "natural" morality may be conceived in any number of ways as the creative response of the human person to life.

Because a historicized natural law perspective concerns human subjectivity and agency, other disciplines such as sociology, anthropology, and psychology are likewise granted warrants for admission as sources of moral reflection. Study and description of the concrete aspects of human behavior are not viewed in opposition to a monolithic, all-encompassing philosophical system but are respected as sources of moral anthropology on their own terms. In contrast to the church's traditional use of natural law as a "closed system" explaining all features of human life,

> philosophy must admit that it never adequately captures man's total experience, and therefore, cannot be its totalitarian sovereign. . . . For theology has to do primarily with history and the future. While philosophy can consider historicity and orientation toward the future only formally, the sciences focus on the content of history and the future.[36]

Another implication of the admission of historicity is that it calls into question the regular division by the manualists of the "natural" from the "supernatural." This division, as John Mahoney notes, is much more Augustinian than Thomistic in origin and accentuated by post-Tridentine scholasticism.[37] It ignores the theological truth that "there is a supernatural element to nature itself as it historically exists, to which moral theology, with its long indebtedness to Stoic and Aristotelian ways of thinking has not given its attention."[38] To embrace history, circumstance, concrete situations, and experience as incarnational loci of God's activity and not merely as accidents in a predetermined plan for creation is to welcome them and scientific articulations of them into partnership with theological reflection. Rahner concludes:

> It is precisely expressions of faith (and thus theology) in respect of man which must by their very nature involve themselves above all in man's historical situation. This means dialogue with and within this situation in so far as the latter has itself been the object of scientific and theoretical reflection; it also means courage to become involved with the unreflected situation, accepting it and speaking from within it in the Christian hope that the truth of God, which must needs be expressed, will not—by the Spirit of God—be substantially corrupted either objectively or subjectively by being expressed from within the particular historical situation, even when unaccompanied by a final and transparent confirmation as to the legitimacy of the historical situation. It is obvious from this point of view that a complete, self-enclosed theological system is an absurdity.[39]

Other revisions of the natural law perspective do not have this lack of historicity as their central concern. These revisions, too, assist in providing the warrant we seek. A recurring criticism of natural law is its poor accounting for the reality of human sin. This contention, often coming from Protestant circles, is that we ought not rely on human reason to discern a moral course of action, since reason is significantly flawed by the presence of sin.[40] And Curran notes: "Sin relativizes and affects all reality. How often has reason been used to justify human prejudice and ignorance. Natural law has been appealed to in the denials of human dignity and of religious liberty."[41] It is beyond doubt that one of the great assets of natural law, the use of reason, can also be its most acute liability. But the danger resides in the exaltation of reason to the exclusion of other human capacities and spiritual realities such as creation, sin, incarnation, redemption, and resurrection.[42] Accordingly, in the interest of discovering the role of these other human capacities one might include the contributions of social sciences, which have as their focus the forces underlying human behavior—motivation, affection, and socialization, for example. While some Christian ethicists look to scripture as the countervailing source, and others look to a broadened spiritual "stance," this proposed revision may point toward a more comprehensive consideration of "natural" in the human condition—one that abandons simple philosophical views of human functioning and incorporates apprehensions of empirical knowledge. These apprehensions may not explain human sinfulness, but they may at least produce some insight into the effects of sin on the moral life.

A wholesale criticism of the natural law tradition is often brought forward by analytic philosophers as the critique of the "naturalistic fallacy." By this critique, one makes the claim that an "ought," that is, a value, cannot be derived from an "is," that is, from the qualities of a thing.[43] The refutation of this criticism, which goes to the heart of naturalistic ethics, would itself require extended discussion; I will not attempt such a discussion here. Rather, I cite one tack in the refutation that is important and helpful to our discussion.

Gabriel Moran makes the case that we are not looking at the natural law for a single course of moral action, but for what constitutes responsibility to many aspects of the universe, and there are a number of appropriate responses. In ethics, according to Moran, we study not what specific course of action we ought to take, but what courses of action, among the many that are open to us, we ought to avoid or not take because of their inability to lead us to God. We emerge in the end, with the idea that what is unnatural (rather than nonnatural) is what is immoral. On the topic of the naturalistic fallacy, then, Moran suggests that we do indeed look to verifiable (and even statistical) descriptive information about the human condition, but he adds: "As for evaluation, moral issues are not resolved by counting. Nevertheless, a knowledge of how people actually behave is preferable to ignorance when making moral evaluations."[44] In seeking to know the unnatural, we may do well to understand the "counting" offered to us in the empirical sciences.

Finally, we look to a contemporary "revisionist" who directly incorporates the empirical into the natural law tradition, and who does so in a manner quite distinct from other suggestions about the role of the empirical. John Milhaven, whose theories are much maligned because of their rather strict consequentialism, has nonetheless made a strong case for the role of empiricism in the "best of the tradition." Noting that most discussions in Roman Catholic (natural law) circles survey the purpose of certain faculties and then proceed to derive the moral value of such faculties from their determined purpose, Milhaven raises the question of how general the discussion of purpose should be. Should we talk of things as they detract from or contribute to a general purpose for human life, such as a life of understanding and love for self and neighbor, or should we talk of the particular purpose of the faculties of speech or sex, for example?

In either case, we determine the moral quality of things in two ways. Either the act lacks some inherently valued trait such as love, honor, or compassion, or it is wrong because of its consequences, usually designated as "what generally happens" by Milhaven. Discerning the first, he contends, is difficult because direct insight into the hearts of people is not possible in most cases. In the second case, then, what is needed is evidence to find "what generally happens," and this evidence is best offered by empirical science.[45] Milhaven's distillation, although simplistic in tone, represents an early effort to follow up on the promptings of Vatican II church teaching, which we will discuss in the next section.

II. The Evolving Perspective within the Magisterial Tradition

The official Roman Catholic magisterium provides an additional warrant for the use of psychology in moral reflection. Because the evolution of the ethical method employed by the magisterium largely follows the contours of our previous discussion, the recent development of the natural law perspective within this teaching tradition may be roughly outlined by reviewing the features of a revised natural law, some of which I have already discussed: the shift from a classical to a historical worldview, with its accompanying turn toward the subject and away from the cosmos for cues about moral anthropology; a virtual elimination of the clear distinction between "natural" and "supernatural"; an incorporation of human sin and its various descriptions into the discussion of the role of reason in natural law; conscious appreciation rather than apology for the "naturalistic fallacy" that supports the natural law perspective; and the actual assimilation of the findings of empirical science in moral discernment.

In the discussion that follows, I will look to several representative teachings from the Catholic magisterial tradition in order to cite the evolving admissibility of empirical science as a source in ethical reflection. The documentation is drawn from various sources that constitute the body of teachings known as "magisterial" statements: for example, papal encyclicals on social and personal ethics, documents from the Second Vatican Council, papal apostolic exhortations, and statements from the "Holy Office," presently the Congregation for the Doctrine of the Faith. As I am interested in demonstrating a warrant from the widest possible authority, I will not discuss episcopal conference statements or an individual bishop's authority, which I believe already demonstrate the admissibility of empirical science in moral reflection. I have arranged the discussion around features of natural law revision, which pave the way for admission of empirical science in general and psychology in particular.

A Classicist vs. Historicist Worldview

The first feature of revised natural law that is found in the official magisterial tradition is the shift from the classicist to historical worldview. This move from a static, complete, hierarchically ordered universe to a dynamic, historically contingent one is accompanied by a changed moral anthropology. When human history assumes importance as a moral indicator, then persons are viewed not as cogs in the machinery of a predetermined cosmos but as agents who are in the midst of discovering the depths of their own and God's life among them. Change and development are not accidental but substantial. The study of change and development becomes exceedingly significant, as do the data of the physical, biological, and social sciences. The acceptance of history and the use of empirical science are intimately connected. Evidence of such a shift may be found by comparing the body of encyclicals written by Leo XIII with the encyclicals of later popes, culminating in Paul VI's *Octogesima Adveniens*. For the bulk of this discussion, as well as the subsequent one on the turn toward the moral subject, I am indebted to Charles Curran's insightfully developed thesis regarding changing anthropology and method in Catholic social ethics.[46]

Leo XIII's view of the society or state (he makes no distinction between these terms) is a reflection of the natural law tradition grounded in the classicist worldview. Deeply distrustful of notions of equality and participation, Leo XIII is a proponent of the view that a hierarchically established society is an inevitable occurrence, as the "untutored multitude" must be led and protected by a leader charged with its welfare.[47] The historical context influencing such a view included a fear of the power, of liberalism, which Leo XIII saw as a direct threat to the well-ordered state grounded in God's plan. Equality, for example, was an unthinkable option which found no place in this classical conception of society dictated by God's law:

> No one doubts that all men are equal one to another, so far as regards their common origin and nature, or the last end which each one has to attain, or the rights and duties which are thence derived. But as the abilities of all are not equal, as one differs from another in the powers of mind or body, and as there are many dissimilarities of manner, disposition and character, it is most repugnant to reason to endeavor to confine all within the same measure, and to extend complete equality to the institutions of civil life.[48]

Leo XIII continues this perspective in *Rerum Novarum,* his letter on the rights of workers, but he also makes a case for certain inalienable individual rights against the power of the state: marriage, private property, and the right to resist socialism. This exception to the state's power as Curran notes, may be seen as "differing degrees of recognition of some freedom, equality and even of incipient participation as anthropological concerns."[49] Indeed, this evolution, the incorporation of teachings on equality and participation, is carried forward by Leo XIIIs successors, Pius XI and Pius XII, who, in their continuing struggle against liberalism and socialism, increasingly stressed the rights of individuals.[50]

In two major social encyclicals, *Mater et Magistra* and *Pacem in Terris,* John XXIII began a conceptual trend that has endured in the social teaching tradition. In both letters, John XXIII notes the vast number of historical variables that must be addressed in the particular situations of the world. Likewise, his successor Paul VI cites a number of specific contemporary topics that require attention in formulating a response to the equitable distribution of wealth and the just development of nations. Curran says that the effect of this move toward history, context, and particularity was to lessen the impact of the "social doctrine" of the church—"the vision of the plan deductively derived from natural law and proposed authoritatively by the church magisterium"—and to augment a tendency to "begin with the signs of the times and with an analysis of the contemporary situation and not with some abstract principle divorced from historical reality."[51] Indeed, "reading the signs of the times" becomes the cautiously promulgated method employed in the foundational Vatican II document about the church, *Gaudium et Spes.*

This shift toward historical consciousness is best demonstrated in Paul VI's letter entitled *Octogesima Adveniens,* commemorating the eightieth anniversary of *Rerum Novarum.* In the letter, full recognition is granted to a historical method of formulating moral teaching from the demands of unique situations and the base of "the Gospel's unalterable words," even though individual Christian communities may look to former church teaching to "draw principles of reflection, norms of judgment and directives for action." The letter asserts that

> it is up to these Christian communities, with the help of the Holy Spirit, in communion with the bishops who hold responsibility and in dialogue with other Christian brethren and all men of goodwill to discern the options and commitments which are called for in order to bring about the social, political and economic changes seen in many cases to be urgently needed.[52]

The words "dialogue," "discern," "options," and "change" signal the admission of historicity in method to which we have been referring. The implied view of the human is a fluent, developmental one; and the pressing need to read the changing world suggests a ready admission of the sciences as sources for moral reflection, despite warnings about a "new positivism" based on science and technology, as well as about humanity being "imprisoned within [its] own rationality" or its becoming the "object of science."[53] A concluding section of *Octogesima Adveniens* makes an optimistic claim about the role of science to assist the church's articulation of "a global vision of man and the human race":

> Should the Church in its turn contest the proceedings of the human sciences, and condemn their pretensions? As in the case of the natural sciences, the Church has confidence in this research also and urges Christians to play an active part in it. Prompted by the same scientific demands and the desire to know man better, but at the same time enlightened by their faith, Christians who devote themselves to the human sciences will begin a

dialogue between the Church and this new field of discovery, a dialogue which promises to be fruitful.[54]

A Turn from the Cosmos to the Person

The shift from the classicist to the historical worldview illustrates a turn away from the cosmos and toward the person as the gauge for the moral life. In Leo XIII, the universe represented the eternal (and static) will of God to which all reality must be conformed. It is understandable, then, that he would be wary of the notion of equality, as inequality of ability and power was determined by the divine structure of the universe. Likewise, the notions of personal freedom and individual conscience were incompatible with the universal will of God in the cosmos. As Curran has noted, "The only true meaning of the freedom of conscience [was] the freedom to follow the will of God and to do one's duty in obeying his commands."[55] *Rerum Novarum* seemed to hint at some autonomy for the individual as it called for the rights of the individual in the face of two perceived evils, socialism and liberalism. Forty years later, when Pius XI wrote *Quadragesimo Anno* to commemorate Leo's letter on the rights of workers, he included an allusion to the dignity and rights of the individual as a means to fend off the influence of communism. Pius XII continued the move toward a recognition of the person-as-agent by accepting the idea of a limited constitutional state, a bold development when one considers Leo's view of the state (the ruler) as protector and promoter of the cause of the "untutored masses." With John XXIII's *Mater et Magistra* and *Pacem in Terris* came the admission of "freedom" as a ground for the human dignity; and a document of Vatican II, the *Declaration on Religious Freedom,* authored by John Courtney Murray, finally proclaimed the dignity of the (individual) human person in the face of coercion by the state.

The dignity of the human person was the centerpiece of another Vatican II document on the role of the church in the world, *Gaudium et Spes.* Significantly, this document's affirmation of the dignity of the person entailed the presence and promotion of equality, freedom, and participation. But for our purpose here, it is important to note the accent placed on the individual conscience:

For man has in his heart a law written by God. To obey it is the very dignity of man; according to it he will be judged. Conscience is the most secret core and sanctuary of man. There he is alone with God, whose voice echoes in his depths. . . . In the fidelity of conscience, Christians are joined with the rest of men in the search for truth, and for the genuine solution to the numerous problems which arise in the life of individuals and from social relationships.[56]

This culmination to the evolution of the turn from the cosmos to the person as the gauge for the moral life is a critical reference point. In it we see the relatively new but central importance of the person-as-subject in the magisterial tradition. The study of the person in all of its complexity is affirmed, as are the various sources (including empirical ones) from which the church may come to appreciate that human complexity.

Thanks to the experience of past ages, the progress of the sciences, and the treasures hidden in the various forms of human culture, the nature of man himself is more clearly opened and new roads to truth are opened.[57]

Obscured Distinction Between "Natural" and "Supernatural"

With the changed worldview and the admission of historicity and subjectivity into the moral realm of the "natural," the clear distinction between natural and supernatural can no longer be made with such confidence. The outcome of revisions such as Rahner's supernatural existential theology is to find evidence of God's grace in descriptions of the "natural" qualities of human life.[58] The blurring of this distinction can be demonstrated briefly in the comparison between two modes of thought evident in the magisterial teaching on marriage. The first one draws hard distinctions between natural and supernatural elements in marriage; the other, by its obvious silence about the distinction and its affirmation of the "graced natural," does not.

In his encyclical on Christian marriage, Pius XI addressed the modern difficulties facing those who seek to live that vocation. Although most of his references in that regard were rather oblique, he did caution against the "chief obstacle" in "restoring due order in this matter of marriage"—"the power of unbridled lust." The antidote is the life of grace, a seemingly sui generis entity that cannot be mediated by merely natural means.

They are greatly deceived who having underestimated or neglected these means which rise above nature, think that they can induce men by the use and discovery of the natural sciences, such as those of biology, the science of heredity, and the like, to curb their carnal desires . . . they are mistaken who think that these means are able to establish chastity in the nuptial union, or that they are more effective than supernatural grace. . . . For just as in the natural order men must apply the powers given them by God with their own toil and diligence that these may exercise their full vigor, failing which, no profit is gained, so also men must diligently and unceasingly use the powers given them by the grace which is laid up in the soul by this sacrament.[59]

By way of contrast, in his *Apostolic Exhortation on the Family*, John Paul II opens his discussion of the family by reviewing a theology of marriage in which he makes no reference to the specifically "supernatural" order. Instead, he conflates the natural and supernatural by accenting marriage as a sacramental covenant, which even in its "natural" expressions speaks of the depth of God's life within the person:

As an incarnate spirit, that is, a soul which expresses itself in a body and a body informed by an immortal spirit, man is called to love in his unified totality. Love includes the human body and the body is made a sharer in spiritual love. . . . Consequently sexuality . . . . is by no means something purely biological, but concerns the innermost being of the human person as such.[60]

The importance of this historically "official" acceptance of the natural as a mediator of God's grace is far-reaching for the life of the church.

Like the shift to the historical worldview and the person as moral subject, the acceptance of the natural as an arena for God's grace implies, too, an acceptance of the study of that natural arena as an important source for illuminating the ways of God. Such study in our time must include the contribution of the empirical sciences such as psychology. Although neither of the letters cited above makes a direct appeal for psychology as a source of the study of the natural arena for God's grace, they, like the previous evolutionary discussions, provide a helpful backdrop and a justification for the use of an empirical science devoted to knowing the characteristics of human life.

A Call for the Use of Empirical Science

Given the evolution of official teaching, an evolution which implicitly provides a warrant for the admission of empirical science, one is not surprised that a direct appeal for the use of empirical science in moral and theological reflection as well as pastoral practice is eventually made.[61] In a directive describing the fruitful combining of Christian doctrine and morality with modern scientific thought, the words of *Gaudium et Spes* provide a final chapter in this development of thought:

> May the faithful, therefore, live in very close union with the men of their time. Let them strive to understand perfectly their way of thinking and feeling, as expressed in their culture. Let them blend modern science and its theories and the understanding of the most recent discoveries with Christian morality and doctrine. Thus their religious practice and their morality can keep pace with their scientific knowledge and with an ever-advancing technology.[62]

Finally, direct appeal is made for the specific use of psychology. According to *Gaudium et Spes*, No. 62:

> In pastoral care, appropriate use must be made not only of theological principles, but also of the findings of the secular sciences, especially of psychology and sociology. Thus the faithful can be brought to live the faith in a more thorough and mature way.[63]

Obviously, we have only used broad strokes in this discussion about warrants for the use of psychology in moral reflection. We have not taken up, for example, the issues of the limitation of the natural or social sciences in moral reflection or the ethical control of science and technology, both of which are intimately connected to this discussion. But having briefly demonstrated warrants in the Catholic tradition for the use of experience, empirical science, and psychology in moral reflection, we now turn to a specific theory of moral psychology, Norma Haan's interactional proposal for "practical" morality.

NOTES

1. Karl Barth, *Church Dogmatics* II/2, ed. G.W. Bromiley and T.F. Torrance (Edinburgh: T. and T. Clark, 1957), 557; H. Richard Niebuhr, *The Responsible Self* (New York: Harper and Row, 1963), Chapter 1; Gustavo Gutierrez, *A Theology of Liberation* (Maryknoll, NY: Orbis Books, 1973; Stanley

Hauerwas, *A Community of Character* (Notre Dame: University of Notre Dame Press, 1981).

2. See, for example, Josef Fuchs, S.J., *Natural Law: A Theological Investigation* (New York: Sheed and Ward, 1965) and Bernard Häring, *The Law of Christ*, 3 vols. (Westminster, MD: The Newman Press, 1961–1966).

3. "Decree on Priestly Formation," *The Documents of Vatican II*, ed. Walter M. Abbott (New York: Guild Press, 1966), Chapter 5, Number 16.

4. Charles E. Curran, "Is There a Catholic/Christian Ethic?" in *Readings in Moral Theology No. 2: The Distinctiveness of Christian Ethics*, ed. Charles E. Curran and Richard A. McCormick (New York: Paulist Press, 1980), 78–79.

5. Charles E. Curran, *Catholic Moral Theology in Dialogue* (Notre Dame: Fides Publishers, 1972), 67.

6. Sturm cites Werner Jaeger's "massive, detailed and classical study," *Paideia, the Ideals of Greek Culture*, Volume I, Second Edition (New York: Oxford University Press, 1945), introduction.

7. Douglas Sturm, "Naturalism, Historicism, and Christian Ethics: Toward a Christian Doctrine of Natural Law," *The Journal of Religion* 44 (1964): 40–51.

8. Timothy E. O'Connell, *Principles for a Catholic Morality* (Minneapolis: Seabury, 1978), 137.

9. Ibid. O'Connell condenses Delhaye, Troisfontaine, Rahner, and Ryan's agreement that the two strains exist in natural law thinking.

10. Ibid., 136.

11. Charles E. Curran, *Directions in Fundamental Moral Theology* (Notre Dame: University of Notre Dame Press, 1985), 130.

12. Ibid., 130–131.

13. Augustine, *De lib. arb.*, 1, 8, 18; *PL* 32, 1231, as cited by John Mahoney, *The Making of Moral Theology* (Oxford: Oxford University Press, 1987), 75.

14. Mahoney, *The Making of Moral Theology*, 75.

15. For a succinct description of background information on Thomas's development of a moral theology, see Albert R. Jonsen and Stephen Toulmin, *The Abuse of Casuistry: A History of Moral Reasoning* (Berkeley: University of California Press, 1988), 122–136.

16. See, for example, O'Connell, *Principles for a Catholic Morality*, Chapter 13, and Curran, *Directions in Fundamental Moral Theology*, Chapter 5.

17. Thomas Aquinas, *Summa Theologica*, Volume I (New York: Benzinger Brothers, Inc., 1947), Parts I–II, Question 94, Article 2, p. 1009.

18. Ibid.

19. This openness to the development of thought becomes very important in our later discussion of the classical worldview vs. the historical worldview. With the incorporation of Aristotle as a contemporary source in his thesis about the moral life, Thomas was much more open to the historical *development* of thought than some would give him credit. Aquinas's use of Aristotle constitutes a dialogue with thought patterns current in his world which suggests a deep appreciation of new approaches to the moral life. Curran points out the irony of Thomistic thought being employed by church hierarchy in the last two centuries for the exact opposite purpose—to establish a

"perennial philosophy." See Charles E. Curran, *New Perspectives in Moral Theology* (Notre Dame: University of Notre Dame Press, 1976), 45–46.

20. Aquinas, *Summa,* Parts I–II, Question 57, Article 5, p. 831.

21. Ibid., 1011.

22. For a history of developments in casuistry following scholastic formulations of the moral life, see Jonsen and Toulmin, *The Abuse of Casuistry,* 122–179, Chapters 6–8.

23. Bernard Häring, *The Law of Christ* (Westminster, MD: Newman Press, 1963), 14.

24. Ibid., 16.

25. Ibid., 18.

26. See Häring, *The Law of Christ,* 23–33, for a complete listing of these moral theologians and their basic theories and methods.

27. For a further elaboration of the following discussion, see Bernard Lonergan, S.J., "A Transition from a Classicist Worldview to Historical Mindedness," in *Law for Liberty: The Role of Law in the Church Today,* ed. James E. Beicher (Baltimore: Helicon Press, 1967), 126–133.

28. Ibid., 130.

29. Jonsen and Toulmin would take issue with this assessment, noting that there is evidence in the period of "high casuistry" for the use of principles, maxims, and rules as well as the use of practical judgment about the applicability of these to particular cases. See *The Abuse of Casuistry,* 256ff.

30. For an excellent discussion of the implications of the historical and classicist worldviews for Catholic moral theology and its development, see Curran, *New Perspectives,* 137ff.

31. O'Connell, Timothy E., *Principles for a Catholic Morality,* 121. The difference between divine *reason* and *will* is significant. As O'Connell has noted, if natural law is a function of divine reason, then it represents "one aspect of that exercise of divine wisdom that is the shape of creation itself," whereas if it is a function of divine will, humans must respond to the will of God as they would to a medieval monarch. Thus, the legal analogy is strengthened.

32. See Dominic M. Prummer, O.P., *Handbook of Moral Theology* (New York: P.J. Kenedy and Sons, 1957), 27–58.

33. See, for example, the methodology often employed in the Sacred Congregation for the Doctrine of the Faith's *Declaration on Certain Questions Concerning Sexual Ethics,* 9: *AAS* 68 (1976).

34. Karl Rahner, *Theological Investigations,* Volume VI (London: Darton, Longman and Todd, Ltd., 1974), 43–45, 52–57.

35. Douglas Sturm, "Naturalism, Historicism, and Christian Ethics," 122–123.

36. See Rahner, *Theological Investigations,* IX (New York: Herder and Herder, 1972), 69, 71–72.

37. See the excellent outline of the history of "Nature and Supernature," in John Mahoney, *The Making of Moral Theology,* Chapter 3. Gabriel Moran condenses the history of this dichotomy by saying that for Aquinas, it was a nature open to fulfillment by grace, for Reformation and Counter-Reformation theologians, it was nature and grace in juxtaposition, and for twentieth-century theologians such as Rahner and deLubac, "grace that is beyond experience bears strong resemblance to no grace at all" (*No Ladder to the Sky* [San Francisco: Harper and Row, 1987], 88–90).

38.   Mahoney, *The Making of Moral Theology*, 112.

39.   Rahner, *Theological Investigations*, IX, 72–73.

40.   Note two discussions of the role of sin in natural law thinking: James M. Gustafson, *Protestant and Roman Catholic Ethics* (Chicago: University of Chicago Press, 1978), 63, and Curran, *Directions in Fundamental Moral Theology*, 123ff.

41.   Curran, *Directions in Fundamental Moral Theology*, 123.

42.   Curran's discussion of the "stance" of Roman Catholic moral theology addresses this problem (Ibid., 5).

43.   See G.E. Moore, *Principia Ethica* (London: Cambridge University Press, 1971); R.M. Hare, *The Language of Morals* (Oxford: Clarendon Press, 1952). For a criticism of Moore's theory, see G.C. Field, *Moral Theory* (London: Metheun, 1921).

44.   Gabriel Moran, *No Ladder to the Sky: Education and Morality* (San Francisco: Harper and Row, 1987), 93–95.

45.   John G. Milhaven, *Toward a New Catholic Morality* (Garden City, NY: Doubleday, 1970), 127–139.

46.   Charles E. Curran, *Directions in Catholic Social Ethics* (Notre Dame: Notre Dame Press, 1985). See Chapters 1 and 2 for full discussions of both the changing anthropological bases and methods in the body of Catholic social teaching.

47.   Leo XIII, *Libertas Praestantissimum*, n. 23, as cited in *The Church Speaks to the Modern World: The Social Teaching of Leo XIII*, ed. Etienne Gilson (Garden City, NY: Doubleday Image Books, 1954), 72.

48.   Leo XIII, *Humanum Genus*, n. 26, Gilson, 214, 215.

49.   Curran, *Social Ethics*, 10–11.

50.   See Curran, *Social Ethics*, 11–15.

51.   Ibid., 20.

52.   Paul VI, *Octogesima Adveniens*, n. 4 in *The Gospel of Justice and Peace*, ed. Joseph Gremillion (Maryknoll, NY: Orbis Books, 1976), 487.

53.   Ibid., n. 38, 503.

54.   Ibid., 503–504.

55.   Curran, *Social Ethics*, 7.

56.   *Gaudium et Spes*, n. 16 in *The Documents of Vatican II*, ed. Walter Abbott (New York: Guild Press, 1966), 213–214.

57.   Ibid., n. 44, 246.

58.   Rahner, *Theological Investigations*, 1 (London: Darton, Longman and Todd, Ltd., 1961), 297–317.

59.   Pius XI, *Casti connubii*, Sections 101 and 111, December 31, 1930, in Claudia Carlen, I.H.M., *The Papal Encyclicals 1903–1939*, Volume 3 (Salem, NH: McGrath Publishing Co., 1981), 407, 409.

60.   John Paul II, *Apostolic Exhortation on the Family*, Section 11, in *Origins*, December 24, 1981, 441.

61.   In keeping with the evolutionary character of the presentation of this section of the chapter, it is interesting to note that as late as 1961, suspi-

cion of psychology as an ancillary partner to theology was evident. The Holy Office issued a "Monitum," presented as a commentary on Canons 129 and 139 but actually a response to a censured psychological theory challenging the status of certain sexual acts as mortal sins. Among its other prohibitions, it stated that "priests and religious of either sex should not consult psychoanalysts unless their ordinary for grave reason gives permission." (Issued July 15, 1961. Translation from *Canon Law Digest*, Volume 5, 196)

62. *Gaudium et Spes*, n. 62 in Abbott, 269–270.

63. Ibid.

3

INTERACTIONAL PSYCHOLOGY AND MORAL REFLECTION: Norma Haan's "Search for Practical Morality"

Moral Grounds and the Contours of the Theory

The prospect of informing practical theology with empirical knowledge is an engaging one. Given that possibility, we now focus on Norma Haan's interactional proposal for a "practical morality" as a promising base on which to build our theory and practice. We will examine closely the features of her proposal that have bearing on our project. If the challenge is to conceive of pastoral moral discernment in a way that accounts for personal history, emotions, creativity, relationships, and community, for example, Haan's work serves us well as an apt conceptual centerpiece.

The fundamental tenet of Haan's theory of morality is that moral action and development are common everyday occurrences. Morality is not a grand theory whose features we learn. It is not a set of discrete practices that we assimilate and predictably act out in our lives or a special procedure reserved for people of advanced logical and deductive powers. Morality, according to Haan and her associates, is encountered in even the most pedestrian activities of human life, even in simply relating to one another.

This tenet confirms our best suspicions and insights. The moral life is not optimally tested and described in terms of moral crises, impeccable logic, superior cognition, or access to philosophical secrets. It is not simply the domain of those who practice religion or embrace a consciously articulated philosophy of life. We seem to know this. We often find ourselves inspired by the moral impulses and actions of people who are strangers to religion and philosophy and we begin to sense, if only in a visceral way, that morality cuts across lines of age, gender, cognitive development, social class, and personal ideology. As other psychological and philosophical theorists of morality have come to understand, restrictive notions of morality can often be contradicted by common sense. There are saints who may test at "Stage Four" of Kohlberg's scheme, and scoundrels whose formal operational thinking is of the highest order. This insight is the foundational premise of Haan's work.

If morality is encountered as an everyday occurrence, if it is the very water in which we swim, what then is the "content" of this occurrence, according to Haan? The content of morality and the object of Haan's study is the quality of human social interchange. Haan contends that by the quality of our social interchange we can determine the adequacy of our morality. In stating this openly, Haan has chosen a certain theory of value, a moral ground on which to stand, a place from which to investigate morality empirically. Many moral philosophers charge that Haan's move constitutes the cardinal sin in moral theory, namely, the naturalistic fallacy. Haan agrees. Psychology, she argues, is engaged by a prior question, "What is morality?" Philosophers are preoccupied by the motivation for morality and check themselves about preferred points of departure such as the greatest good, the categorical imperative, or justice conceived behind a veil of ignorance; psychologists seek the "practical, everyday morality that given the opportunity, all people would presumably endorse as the way they would ideally act."[1] Psychologists, then, can capitalize on the methods presumed in an empirical enterprise and state openly, albeit provisionally, a premise to be tested. Haan outlines guidelines for any psychological research about morality:

> First, the naturalistic fallacy must be committed, and a tentative, working formulation of moral grounds that is forever open to revision, refinement and abandonment must be chosen. Second, we assume that the social scientist's special task is to discover, describe and explain the practical morality that people and societies actually idealize. Third, we assume that social scientists' effort will be more fruitful and society will be better served if a universal morality—if such exists—is the target of their work.[2]

Thus, the enterprise of psychologists according to Haan is the search for "thin" assumptions of value, rather than the "thick" ones that philosophers propose and criticize.[3] That is, psychologists are not engaged by "best" theories but by "true" ones, and their object of study is the depiction of a common operative morality. While best theories propose specific values and principles by which one should live, true theories describe the basic boundaries within which all people perform in moral situations. While a philosopher often argues his or her best theory by demonstrating its superior premise or elegant logic, the psychologist may argue for the adequacy of a true theory based on its ability to describe a universally existent phenomenon.

In this case, Haan seeks to describe a true theory of common morality. Since what is at stake is morality itself, values are, of course, involved, and one must concede that thin values, which elicit wide agreement, are present. All such description could well be a misguided project if no such common morality, even of the thin kind, exists. But as Haan states, "to assume otherwise before the work is done would seem to be a failure of scientific nerve."[4]

In addition to these methodological convictions, Haan emphasizes the need to bear out her theory by studying moral action as opposed to moral reasoning. With this emphasis she departs from other theorists, who are content to consider reasoning and speech, for example, as the principal determinants of morality. Sharing her conviction with the social-learning perspective on morality, she defends action as the primary gauge:

> Action is regarded, in everyday life, as the only authentic criterion of moral truth. Understanding the conditions for the disparities between what people think and what they do could lead to understanding moral default, callousness, and courage. Although many societies have attempted to hold people morally responsible for their thoughts, programs of thought control invariably fail or are imperfectly enforced. Reported thoughts are readily simulated; authentic thoughts become private and the controller finds that evidence is inaccessible.[5]

Having outlined the general contours of Haan's method, let us turn to a discussion of the content of her social interaction proposal of morality. The foundational concept on which her other assertions rest is that practical morality consists of social interaction, which in the theory is articulated as dialogue. Haan asserts that moral dialogues occur at all times, filling our lives with endless negotiations of positions, claims, convictions, rights, and feelings, to the point that we may be unaware of them. These negotiations may be between two people, within the ambivalent mind of a single person, between a person and a society, or even between societies. In the course of these dialogues, we come to know and develop our capacity for achieving some equitable balance with others who are likewise engaged. A common pattern for the commencement, conduct, and resolution of this dialogue might be the following: Some "moral contretemps" occurs that draws the attention of both parties (or positions, in the case of one ambivalent mind), such that discussion must occur. This discussion is executed in good faith, and a balance or equilibrium is established or restored.[6]

That both the quality of the discussion and its outcome are the determinants of morality is a distinguishing feature of the theory. In its practical, everyday consideration, morality is as much the process of achieving equilibrium as the final outcome. Discussions conducted in bad faith or defensiveness, for example, even if they result in some mutually agreed-upon course of action, do not genuinely qualify as establishing or reestablishing the desired moral outcome, equilibrium. True "equalization" occurs when participation is at a maximum, when all parties can freely contribute to the exploration and resolution of the issue at hand.[7] Forging the equitable outcome is a complex matter of attentive respect for all dimensions of the discussion—the issue, the context, and the participants. As such, emotions and context, for example, play critical roles in the social interactional proposal; their importance in the process of equalizing and in the outcome of equalization is an accepted element of the theory.

> For one person to understand another, attitudes of receptivity and amity are required; people must cast their self-preoccupation aside. The dialogue persuades and corrects both parties despite their initial intentions. Typically, each party brings out cognitive-affective considerations. Sometimes people prefer and choose the best rational-cognitive argument (such is our commitment to logic and reality), but the objective circumstances do not always override the emotional importance of less rational views.[8]

As with any dialogue, the parties cannot be invested in "winning," lest the process be completely subverted. Haan is quick to point out that the dialogue is conducted as much to discover points of agreement and similarity as it is to discover points of contention and difference. In a discussion marked by true equalization, "losing" is not moral "deficiency" as it is in moral theories of "thick" assumption. Haan demonstrates this distinction in her explanation of equalization:

In the best circumstances, the achieved balance rests on the parties' creation of equity because they discover that they have common interest. But other balances are workable: compromises of advantages, wherein all receive smaller advantage than they initially wanted; compromises of disadvantages, wherein all suffer some disadvantages; or choice of the lesser of two evils. In real life solutions are often rational, which is not always the same as their being logically impeccable. Given the complexity of human interchange and the unique needs of each person, we all expect to suffer occasional minor injustice, if it is not perpetuated and if it is the only nearly rational solution available.[9]

Losing is "not necessarily devastating to participants, because being wrong concerns what a person is doing, which can be merely mistaken or foolish and not necessarily immoral."[10]

Haan's interactional proposal, unlike other psychological and philosophical moral theories which presuppose that morality consists of checking unbridled self-interest and accounting for others' claims according to preestablished principles, openly acknowledges and promotes self-interest as a key factor in genuine equalization. One of the starting points for the theory, as Freud has noted, is that persons naturally want to consider themselves as moral beings. As a practical concern, a genuine dialogue, the essence of morality, cannot ensue unless parties commence on terms of equal regard. Concessions that are gifts ultimately undermine equalization:

That selves must guiltlessly receive their deserts in order to function givingly is an insight of modern psychology. If the self is not adequately considered by the self and if the self does not require the other to consider the self's claims, the stage is set for morally corrupt, masochistic relations . . . balances cannot be achieved by benevolence. Thus, we can see why the magnanimity of the welfare state morally violates rather than pleases its recipients; instead of gifts, people much prefer what is legitimately theirs.[11]

This outline of the foundational concept of morality-as-interaction offers a starting point for an exposition of Haan's theory. In order to explicate the content of the interactional proposal more fully, we will look closely at two major topics within the theory, moral development and moral action.[12]

Moral Development and Action

One of the distinguishing features of moral development as conceived by the interactional proposal is that young children are viewed

as "morally naive but immediately induced to participate recipro-
cally." Quite simply, this very positive view of humanity is offered in
contrast to other theories that stress childrens' virtual neutrality or
egocentricity. The word "naive" suggests a much more hopeful state
in which the person begins life. Growth is not an ordeal of controlling
impulses but a matter of discovering the advantages of reciprocity
and cooperation. Indeed, the movement in moral development is
described as a "gradual progression toward more complex, discrimi-
nating dialogical skills," as opposed to movement through an invariant stage sequence culminating in the most "adequate" conception of
justice. Development is clearly an accrual of social skills through
social and emotional experience, rather than an increase in one's
capacity for logic, as most cognitive theories maintain. Consequently,
social interchange assumes great importance as the necessary but not
sufficient condition for moral development, and the limiting condition for development is the total lack or thwarting of participation in
social interchanges.

What emerges is a portrait of development that is highly fluid and
dependent from the initial stages on the quality of interaction in the
life of the agent. All development is interactional, that is, it depends
on the quality of dialogue. Therefore, it can only loosely be outlined
in stage form because, as Haan notes,

> ... moral skill occurs as forms of dialogues and solutions
> achieved earlier are reused, but most often revised, modified, or
> elaborated in new dialogues. This "creative," inductive, particu-
> larized quality of moral discussion and solution makes it highly
> unlikely that the development of moral skill is accurately charac-
> terized by successively structurally homogeneous stages.[13]

The "vehicle of change," the opportunity for development, in
this scheme of moral development is social and intersubjective disequilibrium; that is, some kind of interpersonal stress or upheaval
puts in motion the agent's accrued dialogical skills and challenges the
agent to create new skills to respond to a particular situation. Rather
than using moral principles from a past tradition as the major premises from which courses of action may be deduced, the agent reinter-
prets and incorporates historic moral principles according to the
creative dialogue about a solution for a given context and situation.

Similarly, we can characterize the social interactional proposal's
view of the conditions for moral action. The context of that action, as

we have seen, is a dialogue in which the parties openly consider the particular features of a situation. The dialogue proceeds through an inductive clarification of the positions, issues, and emotions of all parties involved, with everyone's conscious and free participation. The determined course of action is the agreement, the moral balance forged by the process of the dialogue. Emotions play an important part as the essential conditions that facilitate or deter the action of equalizing. In fact, an agent's experience of stress or a situation's potential for creating moral oppressiveness can undermine or inhibit effective action.[14] The motivations for action are the maintenance and promotion of the view of the self as moral, as well as the relatively uncomplicated desire to enhance relationships with others. The social stipulation of the opportunity for full participation of all members of the dialogue ensures moral action. Haan lists three capacities for genuine moral action according to the scheme: the persons' level of moral skill; the open nature of the dialogues (i.e., all contributions and expectations are openly articulated and understood); and the practicality of the particular solutions that match the demands of the situations.[15]

Coping and Defending

Open exchange and participation are of paramount importance for both moral action and development in the social interactional proposal. Emotions, whether articulated or unarticulated, are also key factors in moral exchange and participation. The interactional proposal posits that morality is more emotionally charged than a rational calculus. Haan calls it a "hot" rather than "cool" cognition. What, then, is the precise role of emotions in the interactions from which development and action flow?

To answer this question, Haan focuses her attention on the function of defense mechanisms in moral exchange. Borrowing the defending functions from Freud's theory of ego defenses for the "id," and supplementing these with corresponding "coping" techniques, Haan develops a theory to accompany the interactional proposal that explains the role of stress and emotion in moral interaction. A common occurrence is that people experience stress in encountering a situation requiring moral discernment. Although that stress can actually assist them toward good discernment by heightening their awareness, involvement, and participation, often the defenses connected to such stress prevent or obscure a "coping" with the particular situation that would serve sound discernment much better:

> When people cope with stress, I mean that their considerations and choices of actions are likely to be more apt, differentiated, and sensitive. When people defend themselves, they are more likely to distort and become diffused, rigid, and obtuse. Thus a major hypothesis of our research has been that levels of moral adequacy will rise when people cope and fall when they defend.[16]

"Coping" and "defending" are not merely descriptive of moral discernment. They describe actions that people "characteristically or immediately take to solve problems."[17] I will not attempt a full explanation of the "coping and defending" thesis here.[18] Rather, I will note briefly some significant properties of the two types of ego processes, so as to develop a critical method for pastoral moral discernment. Haan's "pivotal assumption" about people's temporary use of coping and defending techniques is important to our thesis: "People will cope when they can, simply because coping works better, but they will defend if they must in an overpowering situation."[19]

The coping processes that people employ to solve moral dilemmas interactionally are generally characterized by the following properties: choice and flexible behavior. Coping pulls toward the future but takes account of present needs and the requirements of the situation. It involves a differentiation of thought that promotes the separation of elements for consideration, and it allows for the satisfaction of affects in open ways, especially disturbing affects that are expressed but "metered." Defending, on the other hand, involves turning away from choice and thereby favors rigid response. It is not future-oriented, but pushed from the past; it tends to distort the consideration of a situation's present elements. It characteristically involves undifferentiated thinking and takes in unrelated elements for consideration. There may be attempts to achieve affective satisfaction by defending and thereby creating a subterfuge of the situation. There is also a mistaken assumption that disturbing feelings will "magically" disappear.[20]

Haan outlines ten of these coping and defending processes, dividing them into four classifications: cognitive processes by which people reason, reflexive-intraceptive processes by which people interact with their own thoughts and feelings, attention-focusing pro-

Taxonomy and Examples of Ego Processes*

	Modes	
Generic Processes	*Coping*	*Defending*
	Cognitive Processes	
Discrimination: Separates idea from feeling, idea from idea, feeling from idea	**Objectivity:** "I am of two minds about this problem."	**Isolation:** "There is no forest, only trees."
Detachment: Lets mind roam freely and irreverently, speculates, analyzes	**Intellectuality:** "My past economic insecurities have led me to a degree of petty stinginess."	**Intellectualizing:** "My stinginess can be explained by my upbringing."
Means-end symbolization: Analyzes causal texture of experiences and problems	**Logical analysis:** "Let's start at the beginning and figure out what happened."	**Rationalization:** "I was trying at first, but one thing after another happened."
	Reflexive-intraceptive Processes	
Delayed response: Holds up decision in complex, uncertain situations	**Tolerance of ambiguity:** "There are some matters that can't be resolved when you want them to be."	**Doubt:** "It's the decisions that get me; I don't know what will happen if I choose to do it."
Sensitivity: Apprehends others' reactions and feelings	**Empathy:** "I think I know how you feel" (second person agrees that first speaker does).	**Projection:** "Don't think I don't know what you have in mind" (second person surprised and mildly guilty).
Time reversion: Recaptures and replays past experiences—cognitive, affective, social	**Regression—ego:** "Let's brainstorm this for a while."	**Regression:** "I just can't deal with this; I'll just give up."

cesses, and affective-impulse regulating processes by which people regulate emotions and feelings. (*See* the Table above.) This scheme begins to describe the range of discernment techniques employed by people of varying personality traits. "For example, intellectuals often cope cognitively with objectivity, intellectuality, and logical analysis, whereas artists characteristically cope more emotionally with sublimation, substitution, and suppression."[21] Other extrapolations based upon extroversion and introversion, for example, seem quite pos-

TAXONOMY AND EXAMPLES OF EGO PROCESSES *(Continued)*

	Modes	
Generic Processes	*Coping*	*Defending*
	Attention-focusing Processes	
Selective awareness: Focuses attention selectively	**Concentration:** "I intend to work on this job now, and I'll worry about that later."	**Denial:** "Every cloud has a silver lining, so there's no reason to be concerned."
	Affective-impulse Regulating Processes	
Diversion: Emotions expressed	**Sublimation:** Person expresses emotions, both positive and negative, toward objects, people, and activities in relevant and understood ways	**Displacement:** Person displaces emotions from the instigating situation to express them in another situation of greater safety
Transformation: Primitive	**Substitution:** Person appears to have thoroughly and comfortably transformed uncivil feelings into their socialized forms	**Reaction formation:** Persons reactions are so socialized that they seem strained, excessive and brittle
Restraint: Emotions restrained	**Suppression:** Person restrains emotions when their expression would be dysfunctional, but knows what she or he feels and what she or he is doing	**Repression:** Person curtails cognitive knowledge and reactions, irrespective of her or his condition and the situation, but emotions are free-floating

*Reprinted by permission of New York University Press from *On Moral Grounds: The Search for Practical Morality* by Norma Haan, Eliane Aerts, and Bruce Cooper, in collaboration with Kendall J. Bryant. © 1985 by New York University.

sible. It would also be interesting to determine whether characteristic coping processes are accompanied by directly corresponding defending processes or whether there would be a crossover from reflexive-intraceptive processes to cognitive processes in the case of certain personality traits, level of moral skill, and the type of situation. In other words, does a moral agent who is usually emotionally expressive always defend by doubt, projection, or regression, or does he or she occasionally defend with the more typical cognitive defenses of isolation, intellectualization, or rationalization? Nonetheless, this accompanying theory offers great assistance in our attempt to develop a conceptual framework for describing practical moral discernment techniques.

The Experiments and the Conclusions

Testing these moral grounds has been a complicated matter. The premise of interactional theory is that there are a number of situational and personal factors that influence moral action and development. This premise suggests research designs which are complex from the perspectives of both the psychological professional and certainly the layperson. Given the scope of this chapter, I will provide only a brief overview of the experiments and the applicable conclusions drawn from them.

The theory that Haan and her associates have developed is largely a response to the theory of cognitive development, particularly that advanced by Lawrence Kohlberg. Knowing her dialogue partner helps to explain the constant reference to comparative findings for the cognitive model of moral development. Both her design and her conclusions are often articulated in relation to the design and conclusions of the cognitive proposal.

Because the interactional theory adopts action as the primary determinant of morality, the experiments seek to test moral action rather than strictly moral reasoning. I refer here to three major studies by Haan and her associates. In the first study, Haan recruited a number of friendship groups of adolescents to participate in moral discussions of hypothetical situations and moral games in which subjects interacted with one another. Haan conducted a second, very similar but more detailed, study with first-year university students. Yet a third study was of preschoolers' moral actions and emotions in one of the games that the other groups had played, "Prisoner's Dilemma."[22]

In the first and second studies, adolescents and first-year university students were divided into groups of ten participants, which were relatively homogeneous in personal background and divided equally between genders. An initial interview consisted of an assessment of the participant's "moral level" according to Kohlberg's scheme. Additionally, participants evaluated other members in the group according to personal qualities such as "makes penetrating arguments, dominates, is fair, and is straightforward." After agreeing to do so at the interview, they also took the California Psychological Inventory (CPI), completing and returning it by the first session. Some of the groups then played moral games which involved differing amounts of personal stress, while others engaged in discussions of hypothetical moral dilemmas. A typical moral game was "Starpower," in which

> Players were randomly divided into three initial subgroups, identified as the Circles, Triangles, and Squares. They individually traded chips of different colors and values to achieve series of chips that were worth varying numbers of points. Players with more points moved to the "highest" of the three subgroups, the Squares. After several trading sessions, the leader passed control of the game over to the Squares, who then invariably imposed new oppressive rules. As a result, they unthinkingly constructed, to their own advantage, a three-tiered society where possibilities for "socioeconomic" mobility soon vanished. Play usually ended with the lower groups rebelling and refusing to play. The essential moral issue was the conflict between the self-serving stance of the Squares as opposed to the plight of the lower groups, the Triangles and the Circles.[23]

A typical hypothetical dilemma was the following:

> At the end of routine questioning by an FBI agent about a security clearance for a former roommate, Bill is asked whether his roommate had ever been involved with illegal drugs. Bill recalls that one time—and one time only—his roommate came in late, very excited because he had just earned $500 for delivering heroin from one address to another. Should Bill tell the FBI agent?[24]

Although a staff person facilitated the gaming sessions, the course of the game was determined by the participants. The discussion sessions were conducted by a staff leader who followed procedures outlined by Kohlberg's method of moral "education," exposure to higher levels of reasoning. In both cases, a number of other trained staff members assigned numerical valuations to particular group dynamics in order to measure the collective variables leading to moral action and growth.

Of special interest to the eventual interpretation of the findings was the characterization of given groups as "led" groups, that is, those whose proceedings were led by a member of the group who had received high ratings from peers for leadership and fairness, and "dominated" groups, that is, those whose proceedings were dominated by a member of the group who had received a sufficient number of "dominant" ratings by peers. Following the series of games and discussions, participants returned for a second interview within two weeks of the end of the series and a third interview three to four months later. In both follow-up interviews, participants discussed and resolved hypothetical dilemmas for the purpose of assessing their moral "growth."

In the study involving preschoolers, similar gaming took place. Nineteen dyads of four-year-olds with varying degrees of friendship (as evaluated by teachers) participated in a cognitively simplified version of one of the games, "Prisoner's Dilemma." In the game, each of the players is equally rewarded for equal cooperation with his or her opponent, but each also has the opportunity on a given turn to default on agreements with opponents in order to receive a greater reward than the opponent. Examining the possible moral acts of equalization, reparation, stalemate, default, and betrayal in conjunction with emotions measured by facial expressions, the tests revealed a positive correlation between friendship and sensitive moral action, even though the verbalization skills of the children were limited.

1. Perhaps the most significant conclusion is that in all three investigations, parties exhibited incidences of equalization, reparation, stalemate, default, and betrayal. These regular features of interactional morality surfaced regardless of age. Such results support two theses. First, interactional morality adequately describes the elements of a common, "practical" morality which is a "far simpler but more general and perhaps more fundamental moral impulsion than proposed in other systems."[25] Second, moral "development" is well conceptualized by the interactional proposal as increasing skills of dialogical action rather than by the concepts offered in other theories. Indeed, in commenting upon the presence of the "capacity to operate at morally sensitive levels" in the preschoolers, Haan states that we might attribute a seeming moral incapacity in young persons to mere vulnerability to stress, thus leaving us with the question "What does actually develop in the phenomena we have taken to be moral development?"[26] It may very well be "a) the maturing of problem-solving capacities that then reduce moral conflict and stress vulnerability as well as b) the increasing cognitive and factual complexity of social situations wherein the young are expected and themselves

expect to act. In this case it could be that the young only seem to have increased their moral capacity."[27]

2. Students who participated in led rather than dominated groups and students who "coped," that is, avoided defensiveness, had higher interactional and lower cognitive moral scores. Haan's interpretation is that

> Interactional morality seems to describe the ways these students acted when their circumstances were optimal and when they could cope. Interactional morality may therefore be the way that people prefer to deal with moral problems.[28]

In addition, it was noted in the groups that a number of the men had very high cognitive scores when they were under stress, and that low interactional scores accompanied these cognitive scores. Two interpretations follow from this. First,

> Although interactional morality may be closer to the morality that people cherish, cognitive morality may be the method some people use when they are personally threatened.[29]

Second, in regard to the correlation between cognitive morality with men and interactional morality with women,

> In action situations, the women seemed to use either form of morality, whereas some men who are characteristically defensive, had higher cognitive scores when they were stressed.[30]

The second finding is of great interest to those who are currently studying the relationship of higher levels of cognitive morality with the male gender.

A current widespread criticism of Kohlberg's scheme is that because the theory was tested with an all-male sample, it does not account for a possible difference in women's moral decision making. Carol Gilligan has noted such a difference in her studies of women seeking abortions and has ascribed the consistently "lower" moral levels among women to a differing operative morality for women, to an ethic of "care and responsibility" that eludes measurement by Kohlberg's standards.[31] Haan's finding is less sweeping but perhaps more accurate: Men may be typically given to defending themselves from stress in a cognitive way, and they indeed become proficient at it. But this reaction may have as much to do with personality-related responses to stress as with gender. Haan's research suggests that there are other ways than Gilligan's ground-breaking attempt to explain the phenomenon prompted by Kohlberg's theoretical deficiencies. As Norma Haan once told me of Gilligan's theory, "I am suspicious of any morality which puts one half of the population at odds with the other."

3. Four other conclusions are worthy of our specific attention.[32] First, according to moral ratings done by outside observers, students who coped and avoided defensiveness had higher moral action scores. Clearly, the interactional mode of dialogue produces significantly higher moral action scores. Second, of the ten coping and defending ego processes, certain processes were consistently associated with moral action in positive and negative ways. They included "intellectuality (a free consideration of possibilities), empathy, and suppression (not repression) of emotions; and negatively: isolation (separating related facts [from] facts or related feelings), intellectualizing, and displacement (taking negative emotions out on others)."[33]

> In other words, higher moral action occurred when the young people considered all possible solutions within the context of being concerned for their protagonists and regulating their own feelings. At the same time they needed to get the situation "together" in their minds on a real, not intellectualized basis and refrain from accusing their protagonist for their present difficulties.[34]

Haan concludes, then, that a certain kind of dialogue produces moral action. But not just any dialogue will suffice toward that end. For example, a shouting match between two intransigent parties would seem to encourage precisely those processes negatively associated with moral action. Such "dialogue" at the very least inhibits moral action and may actually thwart it.

Third, two situational factors had correlations with higher moral scores in the gaming sessions for the first-year university students. Scores were higher when the premises of the game were distant from the experience of the student and vicarious in nature. No correlations were significant for discussions. As we might know intuitively, this scientific conclusion suggests that while in the crucible of immediate and personally involving circumstances, people may discern a course of action much differently than if they had the luxury of coolly considering the problem from the stance of the "armchair quarterback." Finally, the game groups that were designated by group members and outside evaluators as "led" (facilitated by leadership skills inherent in all the members) were "consistently more integrative and communal," while the dominated groups (dominated by one or more members) were more "disintegrated and hierarchical in their functioning." In turn, the led game groups consistently produced higher moral action scores. Group structure had no effect on the staff-led discussion groups.[35] This conclusion suggests that the discernment dynamic, the interpersonal context itself, affects the quality of moral discernment and action.

A Summary of the Interactional Proposal: Content, Background, and Evaluation

We do well to recapitulate and situate the social-interactional proposal by addressing three questions: What is morality and how does it emerge in the person? What are the philosophical and anthropological underpinnings of the theory? What are the advantages and disadvantages of the theory?

In response to the first question, we can briefly summarize the major features of the interactional notion of morality. Morality is primarily the equalization of relations between parties who represent two or more positions in a circumstance of moral judgment, moral action, or both. Those parties may be people, a person and society, or ambivalent positions existing within the mind of a person in the process of discernment. Equalization is constituted by an equilibrium that is achieved through a process of dialogue. In the moral dialogue, parties participate freely in making their own positions known and understood, both cognitively and affectively. Each party, too, comes to know and understand the other's position and responds accordingly. As such, morality is the action of dialogue. More accurately, morality is action responding to action, with the measure of morality resting on the quality of the interaction. This interaction is multidimensional, not only cognitive and affective but also dependent on situational factors, the ego processes involved, and the dynamic of the interaction itself.

Conceived as interaction, then, morality emerges within the person as increasingly adequate dialogical skills of exposition and resolution. These skills are the problem-solving skills that one calls on for any decision. They accrue according to recurrence of the "successful" resolution of circumstances requiring equalization of parties and positions. But that these skills are what "develop" when we speak of "moral development" is still dubious according to the experiments. Nonetheless, the interactionist presupposition is that from the earliest age the child exhibits basic impulses toward reciprocity and cooperation. These impulses are realized and refined as growth occurs in a social setting. Moral responses are constructed by the agent in dialogue and retained as responses that "work." Therefore, social-emotional experience and participation are keys to development. Although one may speak of "levels" that characterize this development, it is a gradual process that cannot be portrayed in invariant sequential stages.

Second, what are the philosophical or anthropological underpinnings of the interactional proposal? As we have seen, Haan joins a movement within the social sciences in which scientists make known the normative assumptions from which they proceed. In this case, she states that the "moral ground" on which her theory stands is the equalization of relationships. Noting "compatibility" with Alexander Sesonske's theory of human duty and obligation arising from membership in a community,[36] Haan claims Sesonske's "ground" as her own.[37] Included in Sesonske's theory are the following fundamental assertions: (1) Obligations arise from situations and are established as people make commitments to each other. (2) We are indebted to communities for the aid we receive and the moral growth they engender. Without them, we could not be human or moral. (3) Rights have no meaning outside of communities. When a person claims a right, he or she recognizes that everyone in the community has the same right.[38] At least initially, then, we can make the statement that Haan's is a social view of humanity; it is by virtue of our participation in relationships with others that we grow and develop.

In addition, by its emphasis on affective, cognitive, and situational factors, the interactional proposal reflects a multidimensional view of humanity. Because persons are conceived as moral actors and responders in this scheme, human moral agency is subjective, creative, and constructive, and persons are free to respond according to the demands of each social situation. Finally, in its stress on the earliest presence of moral impulses toward reciprocity and cooperation, the social interactional proposal proceeds from a positive view of humanity.

In addressing the last of our questions, "What are the advantages and disadvantages of this particular theory?" we can use two criteria: the adequacy of the interactional proposal as it can be judged methodologically and the potential "usefulness" of this perspective regarding pastoral moral discernment. The first prominent advantage of the theory is that it describes morality in terms of everyday interactions rather than in terms of the rarified occasions of moral reasoning that are prompted by significant dilemmas in people's lives. Such use of interaction is not only a sound methodological procedure from the standpoint of moral psychology, it is also appropriately used in practical theology—an operative best forged from the insights of actual living. Haan and her associates have distinguished themselves from other theorists of morality by their willingness to pursue empirically the descriptive question "What is morality?" while others, attempting to formulate best normative theories of morality, have settled for answering the derivative question "Why be moral?" To study the former, to begin with actual, common moral impulses as they are exhibited in the everyday world is, as Haan has asserted, to "rebuild our raft plank by plank while we are at sea."[39] It is a risky venture, subject to methodological revision. But it also stands as an eminently valuable theory, both for its advance of the psychological perspective on morality and for pastoral theology's appropriation of it.

Moreover, this phenomenological approach echoes some of the best instincts of the natural law tradition that we reviewed in Chapter 2. The study of moral impulses and common morality redounds to the premise of natural law. However remotely it is conceived, it is congruent with a traditional Catholic view of ethics. The positive, humanistic approach that accents the goodness evident even in young children is likewise a hallmark of Catholic moral anthropology.

I note only a few disadvantages of the theory from the perspective of the discipline of psychology. First, the studies may not account well enough for the background of the participants. While some biographical information was gathered, one questions whether it was enough to determine sufficiently the stance of the various persons participating in the dialogue. That is, one weakness of the interactional proposal is that it tends to suggest that persons pursuing the moral balance come to the encounter as completely pliable partners in the dialogue. Since one cannot presume a "blank slate" position, the criticism must be taken seriously.

Second, the highest age group against which the interaction proposal was tested was undergraduate students. The claim that interactional morality is the "common" morality may be disputed by those who assert that college-age persons are not sufficiently integrated moral agents to test such a claim. Finally, a limited disadvantage of the acceptability of the theory in Catholic circles is its wholehearted approval of the situational nature of morality. This criticism is a limited disadvantage because in the past decade, the vilifying charge of "situation ethics" has been reduced in frequency and intensity in Catholic circles. Although Joseph Fletcher's thesis provided fodder for Catholic critics of virtually every stripe when it was originally offered,[40] and his particular method of doing the "loving thing" is still found wanting, Fletcher's insight about accounting for context in moral discernment nevertheless has gained in general acceptance among Catholic moral theologians. Nevertheless, a suspicion prevails against any theory of morality that downplays such traditional givens as virtue and character and accents the particular features of moral action. We will return to this theme later in the book.

Implications for Pastoral Moral Discernment

We now look to the implications of Haan's social-interactional theory for establishing a foundational ethic and a critical method for Catholic pastoral moral discernment. What contributions do Norma Haan and her associates make to our project?

The first important contribution of the interactional theory of morality is that it bears out the idea that dialogue is a form of moral action. As we have seen above, Haan has refuted the notion that dialogue is mere talk. Haan insists that the act of dialogue is itself moral activity, that the movement from divergent positions to agreement is more than winning or losing because of moral superiority or deficiency on the part of each of the partners. Equalization is a process and its outcome is morality. This claim is central to my thesis. Pastoral moral discernment as we know it in the Roman Catholic tradition is not simply an opportunity for the minister to pass along the moral teaching of the magisterium. The minister is not simply a mouthpiece, but a participant in the moral enterprise that Haan terms "equalization." Theories of moral theology that present pastoral solutions as second-rate moral "compromises" do not account for this fundamental insight of Haan's work.

Haan's emphasis on morality as an inductive activity also has significant implications for pastoral moral discernment. According to the interactional theory, morality is a constructive and particularized activity, responsive to the special demands of a situation through the creative use of historical moral principles.[41] At the heart of the pastoral approach to ethics is the same recognition that particular circumstances must be recognized and respected. Generalizing about an inductive method of ethics without entering the thicket of situation ethics is difficult, and moral norms are helpfully used in applied ethics. However, Haan's empirically based conclusion is that the inductive creation of moral balance is the actual core of morality. This conclusion could serve as a legitimation for pastoral solutions that have been characterized as mere compromises. Far from being a derivative or marginal activity, pastoral moral discernment (in all of its creativity and particularity) reflects a fundamental ethic that cannot be dismissed as mere situationism. By Haan's findings, when pastoral ministers account for context, individual personality traits, and other particular demands of a given moral conflict, they are not evading the tenets of sound moral reflection. They are attending to the very basis of morality.

Another important insight from the interactional proposal is that morality is a social and participative activity. Although this insight may seem obvious, other theories do not ultimately rest on such an assertion. Kohlberg, for example, has constructed his stage scheme such that stages five and six cite individuality and autonomy as the hallmarks of the mature, moral person. Indeed, the occasion for change and upward movement through Kohlberg's stages is cognitive disequilibrium within the individual. Haan, on the other hand, sees the occasion for change and moral growth as social disequilibrium, that is, as some unevenness in relations.

We have seen, too, that free participation is a key factor in creating a moral balance. Lack of free and equal participation is the limiting condition for moral growth in the interactional theory, and Haan has pointed out the implications of this limitation for social ethics and for the education of the young. For example, in advocating "conditions that foster society's and individual persons' moral effectiveness," Haan states that:

from the standpoint of interactional theory, the society in which participation and dialogue are possible is the epitome of moral social conditions. This is not the society of just conditions, benevolently provided or inherited. The means of participation are as critical as the ends.[42]

Even in the case of the parent-child relationship, Haan notes the importance of the children's participation in decision making. She is not naive about radical equality, but she does recall the apt comment of a father who after disciplining his child, said, "We have to come down on her from time to time, but she has to walk away with her moral honor intact."[43]

The social emphasis of the theory fittingly describes the root dynamic of pastoral moral discernment. It is hoped that in a pastoral encounter, the give-and-take of social interaction will provide the opportunity for clarification, motivation, and moral growth. Indeed, "social-moral experience" is the necessary condition for moral growth according to Haan's theory. Logic and deduction are not abandoned in the pastoral encounter, but as pastoral ministers will attest, the quality of the social interaction itself can be a healing and challenging occasion for better discernment and growth.

Having determined the importance of individual social-moral experience as an indicator of moral development and as a requisite capacity for moral action, we might similarly suggest that value be placed on the collective social experience of a community, that is, on the moral wisdom wrought from many persons in common life. Such experience is more than a communal tradition of principles from which rules can be deduced. It is a tradition of a moral wisdom based on the interactions and history of a community.[44] The social model of moral discernment, previously supported only by intuition, now receives descriptive and prescriptive empirical support from Haan.

The stress on free participation and equal responsibility in moral dialogue also has direct implications for pastoral moral discernment. The ethic that guides the pastoral encounter dealing with a moral issue is much more open-ended than that which characterizes the formulation or presentation of moral teaching. In short, there must be genuine two-way communication, assimilation, and integration, and nothing should impede free participation. No role or status should inhibit equal regard for the positions of the parties. The ideal encounter between a pastoral associate and a person seeking pastoral assistance is one in which the dialogue, at least in its early form, is uninhibited by deference to traditional stonewalling tactics, such as citing "the Church's position," asserting that "the Church is not a democracy," or relying on clericalism for legitimacy. Such tactics may be employed by either party, for church teaching or the authority of ordained ministry, for example, may appropriately enter the discernment process on occasion. (We will discuss this further in Chapter 6.) But as expressions of unequal power or obstacles to free participation, they are violations of the moral grounds of this encounter as Haan understands it.

The interactional proposal also places a high premium on the value of self-interest in achieving a moral balance:

> Control of selfishness is the obsessive concern of most theorists. . . . According to the interactional perspective, society's need to control selfishness is matched by its need to facilitate and tolerate . . . legitimate self-interests. In fact, on logical grounds, the theory would fail as a description and explanation of morality if pursuit of self-interest were not allowed. Dialogues would not work and equalized balances could not be achieved.[45]

The pastoral encounter is, and should be, a place in the church in which people express and pursue legitimate self-interest in a moral matter. After all, the personal, individual, particular circumstances of a believer present complications and prompt creative solutions. Haan's theory suggests that the preservation of self-interest is not just a preferred prevailing ethic but a necessity for real dialogue and real moral action.

While these findings have implications for what we have termed the "foundational ethic" guiding the model, other findings have implications for a "critical method," the means of actually engaging in a pastoral discernment that promotes moral action and development. Three of those conclusions are worthy of our attention.

First, the work of Haan and her associates gives credence to the idea that moral actions and moral development are cognitive as well as affective matters. The significant improvement of the interactional proposal over the cognitive proposal of Kohlberg, for example, is that the interactional proposal recognizes that moral "reasoning" (in the broad sense) must take into account a number of other factors, including the emotions, which as Haan has noted, are "essential conditions that facilitate or deter equalizing moral action."[46] This key assertion has strategic implications for a method of pastoral moral discernment. We can expect that the critical method we develop will prompt the minister to consider the affective dimensions of both the moral conflict and the discernment process. The strictly rational assessment or discernment of the moral conflict will be insufficient.

This assertion is borne out specifically in Haan's thesis about coping and defending. The mediation of stress through either coping or defending has definite consequences for the quality of moral action and development.[47] As Haan states,

> Our results consistently suggested that children and people need both personal strategies and social support for dealing with conflict and stress in order to address, rather than avoid and negate, moral issues. Emotional, conflictual and stressful moral encounters fostered development, but only when the group and student were able to cope with these difficulties.[48]

How might Haan's thesis inform a method for pastoral moral discernment? In order to assist "apt, differentiated and sensitive" moral discernment, that is, "coping," the minister would need to be aware of the stress suffered by the individual seeking help—for example, the stress of the moment, the stress of one's background, the stress of remaining moral in one's own and another's eyes, or the stress of resolving or not resolving the conflict. In addition, the minister would have to be a source of support to the one seeking help so that real coping might occur. Although Haan has noted that a person must "defend" sometimes for the sake of self-integration, coping would seem to be the preferred mode in which moral development, discernment, and action take place. If specific coping processes are associated with positive moral action—intellectuality, empathy, and suppression, for example—and specific defending processes are associated with negative moral action—intellectualizing, isolation, and displacement—then the pastoral minister will want strategically to promote conditions for the former and impede conditions for the latter.

Finally, the conclusion from the experiments regarding led and dominated groups is pertinent. According to the interactional proposal, "higher moral action scores"[49] resulted from groups which were led by a member of the group with natural leadership skills, as opposed to those groups that were dominated by a member who violated the rules of interactional morality "whereby all may speak, none should dominate, and anyone may veto."[50] These findings for group process may suggest an ideal role for a pastoral minister who would assist in moral discernment. Although the person seeking assistance may wish to yield completely to the judgment of the minister in a moral matter, the person's moral action and development will be better served by ministerial leadership, not domination, of the discernment process. For example, leadership would entail soliciting and articulating positions in a pastoral dialogue, while domination might be exhibited in an authoritarian teaching or process of editing what is important in the consideration at hand.

As a psychological theory of morality, the interactional proposal of Haan and her associates is of primary interest to my thesis regarding pastoral moral discernment in the Roman Catholic tradition. I stated in Chapter 2 that given the warrants we have established, the contributions of psychology to Catholic moral reflection, though relatively unemployed in the past, are welcome ones indeed. The specific contributions of the interactional proposal are now emerging, including the importance of dialogue and situational equalization in moral reflection; the significance of emotion, stress, and ego processes in moral action and development; and the dynamic of reflection itself as a determinant of moral growth. We will return later to a more detailed discussion of their implications.

What Haan and her associates judge to be the thin assumptions of value in the interactional theory are akin to the normative grounds of others who are more at home making thick assumptions of value in their theories of morality. Moral philosopher John Macmurray and theologian James Gustafson share an interactional base of morality with Haan, even though each is religious in his orientation to morality. With a view toward ratifying, criticizing, and complementing the interactional proposal as an important contribution of psychology to Catholic moral reflection, we now look to Macmurray's and Gustafson's theories of Christian morality as conversation partners with Haan's theory. Although Haan's theory will remain the cornerstone of the thesis, the conversation with Macmurray and Gustafson will contribute to a comprehensive theory of interactional morality strong enough to serve as a base for a model of pastoral moral reflection.

NOTES

1. Norma Haan, "Moral Development and Action from a Social Constructivist Perspective" (Unpublished Manuscript, 1987), 3.

2. Norma Haan, Eliane Aerts, and Bruce A.B. Cooper, *On Moral Grounds: The Search for Practical Morality* (New York: New York University Press, 1985), 44–45.

3. See John Rawls, *A Theory of Justice* (Cambridge: Belknap Press, 1971).

4. Haan, "Moral Development and Action," 3.

5. Norma Haan, "An Interactional Morality of Everyday Life" in *Social Science As Moral Inquiry*, ed. Norma Haan, Robert N. Bellah, Paul Rabinow, and William M. Sullivan (New York: Columbia University Press, 1983), 230–231.

6. Haan, "Moral Development and Action," 7–8.

7. Haan does account for exceptions in this basic theory of equalization, noting that some dialogues are such that equalization simply cannot be the expectation. Of special interest here are the "legitimated imbalances" of the parent-child relationship or persons of inherently unequal power such as physically able and physically handicapped persons as well as nonlegitimated imbalances arising from insincerity of the parties, neurotic interchange, unequal social caste, or the disparity in psychological statuses such as stress. I will later comment on the last of these imbalances, as I discuss one of Haan's central corollary theories, "coping" and "defending" in moral dialogue. For a treatment of the others, see "Moral Development and Action," 12–16.

8. Ibid., 8–9.

9. Haan, *Social Science As Moral Inquiry*, 235.

10. Ibid., 9.

11. Ibid., 19–20.

12. See the outline provided in Tables 4.3 and 4.4 in Haan, et al., *On Moral Grounds*, 67 and 71, respectively.

13. Haan, et al., *On Moral Grounds*, 61. Haan does describe five "levels of interactional morality" that "represent progressively more demanding criteria for identifying the quality of people's moral activity," noting the changes in various features of interactional growth, including the forms of the moral balance, the consideration of self and others as moral beings and objects, the taking of chances on others' good faith, righting the wrongs others commit, overall justification for balance, and reasons for transitions between levels (see Ibid., Table 4.2, 62–64).

14. See the discussion to come on Haan's theory of "Strategies of Coping and Defending in Moral Action," 169–195 in Haan, et al., *On Moral Grounds*.

15. For an example of a conversation which exhibits some of the elements of the interactional proposal, see the "lightly edited" and annotated verbatim conversation among college students in *Social Science As Moral Inquiry*, 220–223.

16. Haan, "Moral Development and Action," 22.

17. Haan, et al., *On Moral Grounds*, 128.
18. For a full explanation, see Norma Haan, *Coping and Defending* (New York: Academic Press, 1977) and "Coping and Defending With Moral Conflict," in Haan, et al., *On Moral Grounds*, 127–140.
19. Haan, et al., *On Moral Grounds*, 131.
20. Ibid., Table 8.2.
21. Ibid.
22. For detailed accounts of these three investigations, I refer the reader to Chapters 5, 6, and 7 of Haan, et al., *On Moral Grounds* and to David Matsumoto, Norma Haan, Gary Yabrove, Paola Theodoru, and Caroline Cooke Carney, "Preschoolers' Moral Actions and Emotions in Prisoner's Dilemma," *Developmental Psychology* [unpublished].
23. Haan, et al., *On Moral Grounds*, 87. See pages 86–88 for descriptions of other moral games.
24. Ibid., 89.
25. Haan, "Moral Development and Action," 37.
26. Ibid., 26.
27. Ibid.
28. Haan, et al., *On Moral Grounds*, 213–214.
29. Ibid., 214.
30. Ibid.
31. Carol Gilligan, *In a Different Voice* (Cambridge: Harvard University Press, 1982).
32. For a complete description of the findings described in this section, see the discussion of "Moral Action" in Haan, "Moral Development and Action," 31–38.
33. Ibid., 33.
34. Ibid.
35. Ibid., 35.
36. See Alexander Sesonske, *Value and Obligation: The Foundation of an Empiricist Ethical Theory* (Berkeley, CA: University of California Press, 1957).
37. It is important to note, however, that Haan, Aerts and Cooper would not say that Alexander Sesonske provides the premise for the interactional proposal, as Judith Smetana has charged in her review of *On Moral Grounds* in *Contemporary Psychology*, 32, no. 5 (1987): 423–424. In a response to the review, they stated openly and succinctly, "Smetana errs in attributing to Alexander Sesonske the premises of the interactional theory we propose."
38. As cited in Haan, et al., *On Moral Grounds*, 26–27.
39. Otto Neurath, as cited by Haan in Haan, et al., *Social Science as Moral Inquiry*, 236.
40. See Joseph Fletcher, *Situation Ethics* (Philadelphia: Westminster Press, 1966).
41. Haan, et al., *On Moral Grounds*, 67.
42. Haan, et al., *On Moral Grounds*, 392.
43. Ibid., 395.
44. James T. Burtchaell has developed this notion of the collective experience of a community giving birth to a moral wisdom which in turn serves as a resource in moral discernment. I hope to develop this idea in a different

way, from the perspective of its moral-psychological rationale, along with theoretical support from philosophical and theological sources. But I am indebted to Burtchaell for the particular term "moral wisdom" as it relates to community experience. See James T. Burtchaell, *The Giving and Taking of Life: Essays Ethical* (Notre Dame: University of Notre Dame Press, 1989).

45. Haan, et al., *On Moral Grounds*, 386.
46. Ibid., 71.
47. See the discussion above on pp. 10–13.
48. Ibid., 394.
49. Ibid., 344.
50. Ibid., 112.

4

PHILOSOPHICAL AND THEOLOGICAL COMPLEMENTS:
John Macmurray and James Gustafson on Interactional Moral Reflection

In this chapter, I will discuss the most salient features of the interactional perspectives on morality offered by philosopher John Macmurray and theologian James Gustafson who, together with Haan, view the moral life as relational, dynamic, and multidimensional. As with the earlier presentation of Haan's interactional proposal, I will conclude each of the two sections of this chapter with the specific implications of Macmurray's and Gustafson's theories of moral agency for an ethical foundation and critical method for Catholic pastoral moral discernment. These three theorists will then return in Chapter 5 as partners in the conversation leading to a foundational ethic and method for Catholic pastoral reflection on moral matters.

I. Relationship and the God of History:
John Macmurray and Interactional Morality

John Macmurray's fundamental conviction is that natural theology, which determines a path to God through common human experience, is not a misguided enterprise. Although it seems awkward to pose this negatively, Macmurray was nearly alone among his contemporaries in defending that conviction. The bulk of Macmurray's thought was published between 1930 and 1965, a period in which modern philosophy was characterized by a marked propensity toward atheism. To both of the predominant forms of philosophy during that time, existentialism and linguistic analysis, Macmurray has a bold challenge:

> I shall content myself, at this stage, with expressing my belief that the more closely modern philosophy keeps to its programme, and the more purely objective its procedure becomes, the more inevitable is the atheism of its conclusion. . . . Yet I cannot accept the conclusion, in spite of its logical necessity. . . . [T]hat religion rests upon some special and extraordinary type of experience apart from which it could not arise—this seems to me hardly credible. . . . Religion is the original, and the one universal expression of our human capacity to reflect; as primitive and as general as speech. It is atheists and agnostics who have been exceptional and abnormal.[1]

As Macmurray perceives it, philosophers of his time met the urgency of a radical "loss of faith"[2] with a lack of nerve and a studied ignorance. Of analytical and existential philosophers, he remarks,

> . . . whereas the logical empiricists discard the problems in order to maintain the method, the existentialists relinquish the method in wrestling with the problems.[3]

According to Macmurray, contemporary philosophy, having settled for theoretical and egocentric method and content, is bankrupt in the face of the modern loss of faith and the diminishment of the role of religion.[4] With no resources to recover either faith or religion, philosophy has become irrelevant to one of the foundational struggles of the human condition. As such, it has minimized the personal aspects of life. Macmurray terms what remains a "crisis of the personal," and he sees his project to formulate a philosophy articulated as a "form of the personal" and to recognize the whole person.[5]

With the portrayal of the human condition in its wholeness as his primary concern, Macmurray challenges the presumption of the "cogito," the "I think," or the Cartesian rationalism in modern philosophy. This, he argues, is what has made modern philosophy theoretical and egocentric. Instead, he proposes the "I do" position of personal action as the reality into which the "I think" is subsumed:

> The "I think" is not ultimate; it is the negative mode of the activity of the Self, and presupposes the "I do". . . . The Self, then, is

not the thinker but the doer. In its positive doing it is agent; in its negative doing it is subject.[6]

This position, as we shall see, is the center of Macmurray's thought. He seeks to give a full account of the human person not just as observer but as participant, not as the subject looking out on the world's happenings, but as the agent of actions in the world, and perhaps most important, the agent who acts in conjunction with other persons. Knowledge of the world is not accrued in order to know of or know about, but to know in the way that one knows a close friend. As such, human action, the core of distinctive human identity, is charged with relationships and emotions. For Macmurray, "all meaningful knowledge is for the sake of action, and all meaningful action for the sake of friendship."[7]

Much of Macmurray's work is devoted to developing an adequate way of conceptualizing human interaction and its moral implications. As noted above, his view of human interaction includes not merely knowing the world as an observer, as a subject, but knowing the world as a participant, an agent. The "knowing" of which Macmurray writes is the knowledge which we have of friends—multidimensional, emotionally intentional, and ultimately active. When we speak of the epistemological framework that Macmurray outlines, we mean a framework for "knowing" in this broad relational sense. Even when Macmurray writes of "modes of reflection," he has in mind this notion that knowing is ultimately an inseparable part of activity:

> Every reflective activity is therefore an activity of expression, which is completed only by an external embodiment. . . . Every student knows from experience how much of illusion lurks in the belief that his problem has been completely thought through and resolved before he has set anything out in writing. Quite apart from this, the incompleteness of the theoretical activity until it is externalized lies specially in this, that only so can it gain reality by becoming a deed, and take its place in history as an act. Publication is essential to the realization of reflection; and we do well to be skeptical of all "mute, inglorious Miltons."[8]

Macmurray also explores and articulates religion as a way of knowing. More specifically, he is interested in a contemporary expression of the relationship between the intellect, the emotions, and religion, as well as the relationship between science, art, history, and religion. As with most of Macmurray's thought, these are connected discussions, and together they begin to offer us a broader perspective on his epistemology. The intellectual and emotional modes of reflection find their unity in religion, which views the Other in community. Macmurray calls religion the "full form of reflective rationality," and the ultimate condition of action.[9] How does he arrive at this formulation? Basing his moral anthropology on the human need for relationships rather than the individual person's ability to grow and accrue habits and virtues, Macmurray contends that the fundamental task of religion is the establishment, widening, and deepening of the experience of relationship in human life, that is, community.[10] But how is religion a unifying way of knowing?

Macmurray returns to his conviction that the person is an agent of action. Further, if we can imagine human history in this light, not merely as a chronology of discrete individual actions but as the intentional action of a single "Agent," we come to a belief in God that is drawn from human history. That is, we come to see the whole of human life not as a series of "events" or "happenings" to which we are passively subjected, but as the intentional acts of a personal Agent (God), acting in relation like ourselves. This vision of the world as personal and communal, of course, requires a certain leap of faith. But human history can lead us to a belief in God and an appreciation for religion as *the* fundamental way of thinking relationally about the world.[11]

According to Macmurray, we can take a different tack to arrive at the appreciation of religion as the wholeness of knowing. In the course of our living and relating to others, we come to know that we are not only apprehending and evaluating the world, we are also being apprehended and evaluated by others. We are both subjects and objects, or, as Macmurray would have it, we are "part of the field of common experience."[12] Moreover, this description of what goes on between us is also an apt description of ourselves before God— "dependent creatures in the world."[13] Macmurray contends that religion, as a way of knowing, rests upon this relational experience one has of the world.

> The focus of all human experience is to be found in our relations to one another. We are parts of one personal world, which is simply the natural world penetrated and transformed by personal purposes. . . . Religion is simply the recognition of this fact and of

its importance, and true religion is its acceptance with all its implications.[14]

Conversation among friends, knowing and being known, is the paradigm for the field of the personal, and the generalized expression of this conversation is religion. The demand for communion from the earliest moment of human existence is absolute and continues until it is perfectly met in breadth and depth. Responding to this, Macmurray explains the place that Jesus has in history:

> He was the religious genius who realized the meaning of community achieved through the history of his own people—the Hebrew race; and in realizing it he made available the universal meaning of religion for all time and all people.[15]

Finally, then, Macmurray would claim that religion, in its widest embrace of "the personal," is "not an aspect of life that can be contrasted with other aspects; it is the integration of all aspects in one whole."[16]

Macmurray's Moral Anthropology

With this preliminary background, we can begin to form a portrait of the moral person according to Macmurray. Of particular interest to us is Macmurray's notion of "self," which will reveal his basic insights about the relationship between action and thought in agency, about moral motivation, and about the roles of reason and emotion in moral agency. As we have noted, Macmurray's thought cannot be isolated from the context in which he lived. Modern philosophy with its own historical biases prompted Macmurray to examine the solitary "I think" position as the starting point for moral philosophy. More specifically, he addressed the formulations of the self which emerged from the "I think" position. Macmurray poses the history of such philosophical formulations. From Descartes to Hume, the self is conceived as a substance, a material that is mathematically measurable and able to be manipulated, that follows the rules of a material order of life. From Kant on, the self is an organic entity, developing and evolving according to the rules of the biological sciences. Each of these periods of history has witnessed its own advances and frustrations in the effort to capture an adequate description of the self. To limit one's consideration to material or biological rules of order and prediction seemed narrow to Macmurray. He set out to challenge those conceptions by developing his own more unified view of the Self, not as substance or organism but as relational person.[17]

The foundation upon which this unified view of the person is built is Macmurray's account of the earliest experiences of human life, best summarized in the essay, "Mother and Child," in *Persons in Relation*. According to Macmurray, the mother attends to every need of the totally helpless newborn as the child educes the action it wants from the mother by expressing those needs. Simply unable to meet such needs constantly, the mother inevitably withdraws attention and care, and the child is left to his own resources, fearful and egocentric.[18] Two paths emerge for the needy child in this fearful and egocentric position: He can aggressively arrange for the care he needs, making the mother afraid of the consequences of not attending to him, or he can withdraw into total passivity to please the mother, thus "winning approval" and the care he desires.

Thus, fighting or fleeing become the alternatives to the child locked in fear and egocentricity. To the child who recovers from the trauma of having been "abandoned," real love becomes possible when he comes to see that he can love and be loved by the mother only by establishing a certain interdependence with her, not through manipulation or passivity, but meeting his own needs along with her.[19] From Macmurray's construction of this early experience comes the relational portrait of the self that characterizes his theory.

To complete this portrait of the self in Macmurray's work, we look to the relationship of thought and action in moral agency. Action is the key category for constituting the self in the relational manner suggested above. The philosophical move from a material or organic conception of self to a relational conception is, according to Macmurray, like the movement in psychology from subject to behavior:

> First, so long as psychology is conceived as a science of mind, consciousness or the subjective, it fails. To establish itself it must think of itself as a science of human *behavior*. Similarly in the philosophical transition, we can no longer conceive the Self as the subject in experience, and so as the knower. The Self must be conceived, not theoretically as subject, but practically as agent. Secondly, human behavior is comprehensible only in terms of a dynamic social reference; the isolated, purely individual self is a fiction.[20]

Why this primacy of action and behavior? What is the specific inadequacy of the "I think" position? Macmurray answers in his core presentation of "The Field of the Personal":

> If we start with the solitary individual, self-isolated in reflection, and consider him existing as a thinker, we do exclude the normal sources of error, and his existence becomes an ideal existence. . . . So we all rise above the sources of error, which lie in the limitation of a spatio-temporal existence and the practical necessities it imposes; above bias and prejudice; above the particularities of circumstance and experience which account for our differences from one another. So we all enter a logical heaven, where there is nothing to sully the pure exercise of reason, and to think is to think the truth.[21]

Obviously, Macmurray does not propose mere action as the distinctive core of the human person. Thought, reflection, and knowledge are complements to such action. Or, according to the above scheme, they are the negative modes of the positive mode of action. But for Macmurray, they are modes of rational activity. So, again, thought falls within action. While action is primary and concrete, thought is secondary, abstract, and derivative; but both are activity.[22] Action may be conceived as "kinetic" activity, while thought, reflection, and knowledge are "potential" activities.[23] All human actions are relational. By virtue of the fundamental relationship scheme which Macmurray defines in "Mother and Child," thought, choice, and action in relationship to an object do not make me a moral person. Thought, choice, and action in relation to another person, and most broadly, in relation to an Other, make me a moral person.

For Macmurray, moral motivation is directly connected to the moral agent's resolution (or lack of resolution) of the mother and child relation described above. For the child who resolves the withdrawal of care as a necessary cue for his own interdependence with the mother, genuine love becomes the "positive" motive in his action with others. That is, the child extrapolates from the relationship with the primary caregiver and makes the desire for interdependence the guiding cause for human action and interaction with others. The child who does not resolve the withdrawal of care in such a "positive" fashion is thrown back upon his or her own resources and, full of egocentricity, develops fear as the motive for action and interaction with others. That basic fear may be translated into actions attempting to coerce the care that has been withdrawn. Those actions, "negatively" motivated, are generally characterized as either fleeing or fighting. Through the fleeing actions, the agent seeks to placate the mother so that approval may be substituted for the care that is missing. Through the fighting actions, the agent aggressively seeks to impose his or her will on the mother, thus frightening her into providing a pseudo-attentiveness as a substitute for the care that has been withdrawn.[24] This negative disposition is self-defense; Macmurray states that it cannot include mutuality:

> Such action is implicitly a refusal of mutuality, and an effort to constrain the other to do what we want. By conforming submissively to his wishes we put him under an obligation to care for us. By aggressive behavior we seek to make him afraid not to care for us. In both cases, we are cheating; and in both cases the *Other* is compelled to defend himself against our deception. Self-interested relation excludes the mutuality it seeks to extort.[25]

Clearly, in this particular case, Macmurray employs the designations "positive" and "negative" to mean more than simple polarities. They also evaluate the motivations he describes. While the positive motivation is other-centered and rooted in love and self-donation, the negative motivation is egocentric and rooted in fear and self-preservation. But they are not of neutral value to Macmurray:

> Now there are two, and I think only two, emotional attitudes through which human life can be radically determined. They are love and fear. Love is the principle of life, while fear is the death-principle in us. I mean that literally; and would go on to explain it by saying that you can divide men and women most fundamentally into two classes, those who are fear-determined and those who are love-determined. The former are not merely dead souls; they stand for death against life. . . . They are the people of whom Jesus said that they need to be reborn. Whereas the love-determined people have life in them. . . . [t]hey are the people who are really alive, of whom it can be said that they possess eternal life.[26]

As we shall see, the motives of love and fear become important in Macmurray's conception of morality, based as it is upon human freedom. Insofar as fear is the "great inhibitor of free action," it must be overcome by the positive motivation of love.[27] For Macmurray, religion has a significant effect on moral motivation.

All religion . . . is grappling with fear. . . . Real religion will save us from our fear but not the things we are afraid of. Therefore any religion, any form of Christianity which offers us protection from life, defense against the consequence of our ignorance and folly and escape from the natural demands of the conditions of our human existence is spurious.[28]

As the domain of the "field of the personal" and the promoter of genuine mutuality and other-centered community, religion casts out defensiveness and its root condition, fear, and engenders freedom and moral action—"life."

Until now, we have said much about Macmurray's notion of thought, especially in relation to action, but we have avoided the term "reason." Macmurray was well aware of the issues surrounding the use of reason in the moral life, issues that pervaded the writings of his contemporaries. One such issue was the respective roles of reason and emotion in human life. On that topic, Macmurray makes several important points.

First, in responding to the "solipsism of theoretical thinking," Macmurray holds that just as the term "person" must be expanded beyond the "I" position to the relational "I and You" position in order to account for both the person as subject and object, so "reason" must be expanded to reflect a human capacity that is both subjective and objective. That is, "reason" must be rescued from the "specialized reference to logical thought," which has contained it in the past. Macmurray explains this development as traceable to the efforts to make reason the differentiating characteristic of the human condition:

The empirical determination of the *differentia* is naturally derivative and variable in principle; and it has in fact varied considerably during the history of philosophy. If it has tended on the whole to have a predominantly theoretical reference, this is because Plato and Aristotle determined the tradition in this direction at the start by their conviction that the good life for man is the "theoretical" life.[29]

But for Macmurray, reason is more than merely the human capacity to assess the outside world subjectively as an observer. Reason must account for the fact that as humans we are assessed by others and respond to them. Declaring that the proper disjunction is not between reason and emotion but between intellect and emotion, Macmurray makes an appeal for "emotional reason," that is, a rational exercise of emotion.[30] As indicated in our earlier discussion, he notes that all actions have motives or intentions that originate in the emotions; and although excess or sloppy emotions may lead to error, emotions

> may sharpen the focus of our attention, quicken our apprehension of the object upon which they are directed, and lead to the recognition of truths, and even of facts, which otherwise would have escaped our notice.[31]

By means of our emotions, or "emotional reason," we come to appreciate ourselves as the object of the other's attention, and thereby, we can appreciate ourselves in an objective manner. Beyond mere subjectivity, "reason is the capacity to behave, not in terms of our own nature, but in terms of our knowledge of the nature of the world outside."[32] As Macmurray points out, this behavior is part of a process of "disillusionment" in which the exercise of emotional reason allows us to act "not in terms of our subjective inclinations and private sympathies," as though our own emotional life were central, but to act in relation to an Other, to "act in the light of eternity," as though we are "part of the development of humanity."[33] Emotion, understood in this light, has everything to do with morality. Through the emotions and "emotional reason," Macmurray has arrived at an objective universalizability of sorts which serves as the foundation of morality:

> Our individual tensions are simply the new thing growing through us into the life of mankind. When we can see them steadily in this universal setting, then and then only will our private difficulties become significant. We shall recognize them as the travail of a new birth for humanity; as the beginning of a new knowledge of ourselves and of God.[34]

Second, emotions serve as the locus of evaluation. Macmurray takes issue with the formulation of the problem of the modern person as a struggle between head and heart. Instead, he says, it is a problem of the heart:

> Our dilemma lies in the fact that we cannot decide what would be the best to do because we cannot decide what is best worth having. That is a dilemma, not between the heart and the head, but

in the heart. What is worthwhile cannot be decided by thinking, by intellect, by science, but only by emotion.[35]

Far from a call for control or repression of the emotional life, Macmurray calls for an increased awareness rooted in the development of "the life of the senses," by which we come to appreciate things in and of themselves and not merely as means to other things.[36] There are pitfalls to such emotional "data"—illusory feelings, feelings that we misrepresent, and insensitivity to feelings that are called for—but in opening ourselves to the life of the senses, we open ourselves to "a real emotional knowledge of the significance of real things."[37]

Implications of Macmurray's Relational Moral Agency

The first implication of Macmurray's philosophy is that it presents and defends a truly relational moral anthropology. As we have noted, for Macmurray, the moral life is the relational life, the quality of our interactions with others. The moral agent cannot be conceived as merely a subject, but is the object of others' moral agencies. The give-and-take between these two subjective and objective realities, between self and other, as Macmurray would have it, is the core of human moral intention and action. His conclusions thus bear out the contention which I made in Chapter 2 regarding the moral importance of pastoral discernment. Far from the derivative or peripheral role that it has been assigned in the Catholic tradition of moral theology, this process of discernment is, according to Macmurray's relational moral anthropology, the very essence of morality. For anyone adopting such a moral anthropology, pastoral moral discernment assumes due gravity in the moral mission of the Church. Specifically, whereas the role of the pastoral minister in discernment with others has been relegated to being a pedagogical conduit for communicating official church teachings, Macmurray effectively challenges that notion by promoting the relational discernment process as a paradigm of moral agency. Parenthetically, Macmurray also casts suspicion on principles and teachings as the core of morality, diminishing the value of blind obedience to principles as the moral "externality" to which Jesus vehemently objected.[38] Moreover, as a particularly intellectual formulation of the moral life, duty assumes an inordinate role, particularly with the ascendancy of principles as the form and content of morality. The significance of emotions in the moral life is thus overlooked.[39]

Emotions are of central significance to Macmurray's moral anthropology. With the emotions serving as a locus for the evaluation of things as ends in themselves, one must necessarily attend to the promptings of "the senses," cultivating an awareness of them. The result of such awareness of things in and of themselves is that through the emotions, we come to know, and not just know about, others. In turn, this emotional "knowing" of others and the Other in an emotional way affords the agent what Macmurray has character- ized as "real feelings." These real feelings (and thoughts) are encour- aged, promoted, and objectified by submitting them to the evaluation of others in a dialogue. To employ more traditional moral categories, Macmurray refers to an ability to get past the trap of self-deception by this intuitive, projectional, emotional means. The unreal feelings that obscure the moral life are illusory feelings, misrepresented feelings, and insufficient feelings. Emotions have both positive and negative moral import that ought not be underestimated. As a fundamental force with which everyone contends, emotional concerns need to be appropriately addressed in their urgency and particularity, and with the gravity they deserve. Specifically, in the discernment setting, the minister must tend to the emotional environment of honesty, openness, acceptance, and genuine dialogue, not merely because empathic regard is an effective counseling technique to elicit self- revelation, but because the fruit of such an encounter is real knowing of a moral kind.

Of special importance are the emotions of love and fear, the cen- tral moral motivations in Macmurray's theory. If, as he has sug- gested, the moral life is positively motivated by love leading to mutuality and interdependence and negatively motivated by fear in its two forms of fighting or fleeing, then the challenge of the discern- ment process, which corresponds to the challenge of religion as Macmurray poses it, is to seek a transformation whereby fear is changed into love. Love engenders a communal morality, an ideal. In the personal, mutual, and interdependent aspects of common life, in the cultivation of relationships, human flourishing occurs. Moral maturity consists in interdependence. Although personal friendship is the "form of the personal," community is the broader moral cate- gory which includes the many friendships that are the forms of the moral life. In the ideal community, each member is positively motivated, heterocentric, a distinct individual "realizing himself in and through each other."[40] Indeed, for Macmurray, this communion is what religion is all about—the genuine communion of persons in the heterocentric (Other-centered), positive mode. The mission of religion is to create, maintain, and deepen this ideal of community and further extend it by the complete transformation of fear as a motive. Macmurray states that this transformation constitutes the "redemptive" dimension of religion.[41]

A realized community, then, is the place of moral flourishing. In a sense, it is the end of the moral life. This notion has strong implications for pastoral moral discernment. Proceeding from Macmurray's assertion that the isolated agent is a self-contradiction, I maintain that moral discernment in a professed community ought never be posed as private activity. For the one seeking assistance in the Christian community, no "case" can be considered without determining both its effect on the shape of the community and the person's involvement in that community. Moreover, the minister, as a leader of the community, stands in the position of promoter of an ethic of mutual relations in community.

Thus, with respect to the actual shape of moral reflection in Catholic settings, the identity of the pastoral minister shifts from the most immediate representative of pedagogical "line authority" to the most immediate representative of the beliefs and relationships in the community, however difficult to determine those often disparate interests may be. This designation may seem to be splitting hairs, as one may conceive of pedagogical line authority as subsumed in the interests of community, but if reciprocity and mutuality are the guidelines by which genuine community is established, then these values must surely be implemented by the pastoral minister. Teaching is only one part of a moral leadership that promotes relationality; listening is the other.

Macmurray attaches deep religious significance to the relationality that undergirds his moral philosophy, demonstrating that personal relationships and mutual dialogue have religious meaning. They speak to us of the God who stands in relation to us in a "personal universe." For believers, the communal ethic outlined above has theological significance beyond mere mutuality with other members of the community. We can discern the movement of a God-who-relates through the moral promptings of the community to whom we relate. For the purposes of a critical method of pastoral moral discern-

ment, the believer is able to detect the movement of God in a relational encounter between the minister and the one seeking
assistance.

This religious dimension is further illuminated by Macmurray's
notion of history, in which the believer sees all history as the action of
God's single intention. The opportunity would be rich for the pastoral
minister to use this idea, even in its abstraction, to establish with
another a religious epistemology, a way of knowing based on faith, in
which God is known in the circumstances of one's life. Beyond an
artificial religious veneer added to a practical discernment process,
such a way of knowing would lend a truly "pastoral" dimension to
"pastoral moral discernment." As we shall discuss in Chapter 5, this
religious epistemology is the theoretical difference, and in the case
of our project, the theoretical advance, of Macmurray in relation to
Haan.

For Macmurray, both reflection and action are critical compo-
nents of the broader category of "activity." He explains reflection as
potential activity, while action is kinetic activity. While the specifics
of the theory are somewhat abstruse, the ascendancy of the "I do"
position in Macmurray makes action the central criterion for moral
anthropology. The implication for pastoral moral discernment is that
in the course of comprehensive moral discernment, the minister
and the one seeking assistance will not only determine the ethical
grounds on which to act; they will also construct a strategy for acting.
According to Macmurray, the explicit rationale for moral discernment
is its culmination in action. Overall, then, discernment is inductive
and practical, responding to the particular demands of the agent and
the situation.

It is evident even from our discussions up to this point that much
is shared between the theories of morality held by Norma Haan and
John Macmurray. We will have an opportunity later to explore at
length their similarities and their differences. Suffice it to say here
that the last and most important implication of John Macmurray's
philosophy is that its close coincidence with Haan's thesis of interactional morality suggests the plausibility of our project, the development of a comprehensive ethic and critical method for pastoral moral
discernment founded on true and best theories. In the strong convergence of their two theses, we see the prospects of a "natural" morality and its practical implementation, grounded in both psychology
and philosophical moral anthropology.

II. Belief and the Moral Community: James Gustafson on Interaction and Christian Ethics

The Interactional Form of the Moral Life

James Gustafson, like Haan and Macmurray, views the moral life as interactions between persons. The moral life is a matter of agents or subjects responding to the initiatives of other agents by taking account of the meaning of those initiatives and then acting according to one's own and others' purposes and intentions. His is a dynamic model of the moral life, by which the agent is open to intervention, resistance, and amendment by others.

How may we synthesize Gustafson's conception of the interactional form of the moral life? As a summary of his reflection on the story that introduces *Can Ethics Be Christian?*, Gustafson draws general conclusions about the form of the moral life. First, moral activity comes about within relationships between persons and other persons, or persons and institutions. Second, these relationships are characterized by a mutuality of dependence and reliability, from which rules and obligations arise. Third, the relationships are not static; and the change that occurs in them is the "necessary condition for the intentional alteration of states of affairs or courses of events." Fourth, the interactions between the persons or entities are somewhat determined by the subjects' relatively fixed limitations and possibilities. Fifth, while that determinacy is true, so is a certain measure of indeterminacy; that is, "What 'I am' is to some extent designatable, but as a result of action and interaction, I shall not be precisely what I am now," and the same is true of "the Other." Sixth, moral relationships occur over a certain period of time and so have past, present, and future dimensions. Finally, persons may indeed be considered as agents capable of purposeful action.[42]

Even though the form, or "conditions," of the moral life can be articulated as interactional in character, Gustafson notes that there are different "grounds" for the interactions.[43] Within the interaction, people use different criteria for judging the rightness or wrongness, goodness or badness of a given course of action. While some agents may employ the criteria of rules or obligations, others may refer to the building and breaking of trust in a relationship, the rights owed to individual persons in a given system, the short-term or long-term consequences of particular actions, or to the morally fitting thing to do. Those criteria in turn give rise to some of the possible styles of moral decision making, such as the simple following of law found in the person-as-citizen; the making of things found in the "homo faber," or person-as-designer; the seeking the morally fitting course of action in the person-as-responder; and the cost-benefit analysis of the person interested in the criterion of utility and consequences.[44]

Decision making is of key importance to Gustafson. We can outline the facets of discernment as Gustafson has consistently articulated them. Good moral discernment, that is, decision making which accounts for the multidimensional aspects of humans in relationships with each other and with institutions, is fundamentally a matter of good powers of perception. It is the ability to "see all that there is," to be "penetrating and accurate in observation" of a situation, the ability to "locate a detail," to be "accurate in perception."[45]

Gustafson begins his explicit consideration of moral discernment by noting what it is not. Moral discernment is not a simple imposition of a model or scheme of analysis. Still less is it syllogistic moves of deductive logic from first principles to particular circumstances, or the accumulation of information regarding the issue requiring discernment. It is instead the careful distinguishing of important from unimportant information and the determination of the relationship of some information to the whole of it and "imaginative inferences" from the information gathered. Moral discernment is not merely emotional or expressive reactions to the issue requiring discernment but also includes supportive reasoning. Finally, it is not a stubborn mode of making a judgment; it entails sensitivity and flexibility.[46] Gustafson broadly outlines good moral discernment as that which "involves a perception of what is morally fitting in the place and time of action."[47] It involves various combinations of interpreting what is truly at stake from the perspectives of the moral participants who have particular histories, backgrounds, and sensibilities "other than rational aspects of selfhood," and coming to comprehend the beliefs, rules, and principles of those participants.[48]

Discernment also strikes the balance between personal "involvement" and personal "disinterest." That is, in the involvement of moral discernment, we engage in interaction with others and perceive things about ourselves and others as moral agents—imagination, possibilities, different natures of the problem at hand, interpretation, sensibilities, empathy. Dispositions are formed, powers and limitations are made known, we gain confidence as moral actors and we see the presence of evil.[49] The rational disinterest or distance of discernment, on the other hand, enables analysis, which "is essential if we are to be cogent in the expenditure of our passions and our other powers to rectify what is judged to be a moral wrong."[50]

But Gustafson's notion of moral agency goes beyond the resolutions of moral dilemmas, even though such resolutions are central concerns of his systematic treatment of the moral life. The discerning interaction occurs between and among agents who are persons with particular enduring constellations of traits that enable and sometimes obstruct sound discernment and good moral action. Gustafson "suggests that it is appropriate to assume some degree of predictability of behavior in persons."[51] Whether this predictability is articulated as "consistency," "character," "integrity," or "style," Gustafson claims that such habitual moral behavior does indeed exist.[52] In providing some account of this predictability, he points to two types of factors—those over which the agent has no control and those which are of the agent's doing. The first set includes genetic endowment, psychiatric illness, unconscious motives, and environmental conditions. The second includes personal beliefs, dispositions, and intentions (both general and specific).[53] Gustafson refers to these factors of consistent behavior as "conditions of the person which persist, which are not whimsical and episodic, and which function in various ways with reference to action."[54] More specifically, they are "conditions which make possible and likely certain sorts of actions without determining in themselves what action will be done."[55] Gustafson distinguishes himself among the three moral theorists in this discussion by espousing this notion of character, or as he would have it, "the sort of person one is."[56]

The Role of Christian Belief in the Moral Life

Gustafson has devoted a substantial part of his writing to the impact of religious belief on the moral life. Though the scope of this presentation does not allow me to convey that thought in its fullness, I will attempt to communicate a general sense of how Gustafson answers the question, What difference does belief in God and Christ make to morality? Having outlined the elements of Gustafson's conception of general moral life, we turn to a broad consideration of his ideas about the influence of religious belief on moral discernment and action.

The most basic assertion about the influence of faith on morality is that faith provides a compelling answer to the metaethical question, Why be moral? In Gustafson's work, the consistent question that guides the moral thought and action of the believer is "What is God enabling and requiring me to be and to do?" Under this general rubric nearly all of Gustafson's thought about the role of belief may be placed. His foundational idea about the believer is that

> The horizon of his vision, both of his responsibilities and of his aspirations, extends beyond the time and space box in which he fixes his moral action for reasons of practical necessity to a power which renders new possibilities and new hopes. His involved discernment is not only in finding what is right and good in the circumstances in which he acts, but in seeking what God is requiring and making possible.[57]

From this guiding moral criterion for the believer proceeds discernment, which aims at a "fitting" action that adequately responds to the judgment about what God is enabling and requiring one to do.[58] Gustafson amends the guiding criterion of the "command-of-God" theologians such as Barth, whose question is "What is God doing?" Gustafson is wary of any unmediated experience of God and views human moral agency, though influenced in believers by convictions of faith, as completely free of divine determination.[59]

This model of the believer's moral life assumes an immanent and communicative God. For believers, this divine communication is encountered in the interactions of human life, where an event is not merely an event, a conversation is not merely a conversation. All human life, but perhaps most especially relations between humans and relations between humans and institutions are occasions of God's intervention in life, enabling and requiring certain kinds of fitting moral action:

> The religious person and community, in its experiencing of the reality of God and believing in God, has another dimension, or horizon, in moral life. In a sense, the relations involved in human moral activity are more "extensive" than appears; the interactions go beyond those we immediately perceive to be significant in the

determination of our actions. In religious language, persons are not only related to other humans, events and to institutions but are related to God in and through these relations.[60]

Because of the significance of human relations as loci of God's manifestations, community, and, particularly, a community of other believers, sustains the faith of the believer and prompts fitting moral action by its ongoing interpretation of the reality of God.

But how does the belief in God, mediated through a community, specifically affect moral discernment and action? Gustafson notes three ways. First, belief in God engenders "senses" in the believing person that in turn give rise to moral discernment and action. Images of God evoke certain dispositions which are then confirmed in the experience of the believer. God, that is, grounds the moral activity of the person by disposing the person in a certain way. These senses of God inform and transform the "consistency," "character," "integrity," or "style" of the believing person by creating certain moral dispositions from his or her images of God. Gustafson shows that biblical and personal images—creator, shepherd, master, king, father, love, and ground of hope—evoke such personal dispositions as dependence, confidence in care, service, obedience, childlikeness, love, and possibility, respectively.[61]

He also specifies six central senses of God, rooted in experiences of God and beliefs about God. He lists these senses, their correlative experiences of God, and the moral qualities they engender by way of "character" formation and transformation: Dependence, rooted in an awareness of God's infinitude and our corresponding finiteness, affords the moral qualities of trust, self-criticism, knowledge of limitations, recognition, and limits to the claims of moral certitude; gratitude, rooted in an awareness of God's beneficence, affords the ability to do for others the good that God has done for humanity; repentance, rooted in awareness of God as a moral authority, allows one to adjust one's moral purposes to the perceived will of God; obligation, rooted in the awareness of God as the one who orders and sustains life, engenders in one a personal and social responsibility that aligns with the orders of creation; possibility, rooted in the experience of God as a source of hope, opposes despair and offers one the sense of opportunity; and direction, associated with the experience of God as *telos*, creates a sense of a path through human circumstances to spiritual ends.[62]

The second way in which the belief in God mediated through a community can affect moral discernment and action is by the believing community's interpretation of the events and circumstances of human life and history through religious symbols and language. For example, a struggle against a particular instance of slavery in human history may be interpreted through the biblical symbolic imagery of "liberation," thus affirming the freeing of slaves by analogy to the freeing of the Israelites from Egyptian rule. Another example may be the interpretation of a specific instance of human suffering and triumph in light of the mystery of the cross and resurrection of Jesus.[63]

Gustafson, however, also recognizes the difficulties inherent in the effort to relate historical events to a religious paradigm. Two prominent difficulties involve the authority of such symbols and the criteria by which one chooses one symbol or expression over another.[64] Gustafson notes that the authority of a particular symbol lies in its ability to disclose the significance of events that may not otherwise have been perceived.[65] It should at least be intelligible, if not thoroughly assimilated, to those outside the particular community employing the symbol.[66] In regard to the criteria employed, Gustafson proposes a multilevel scheme of determination. The symbol or expression should answer to the theological norm of God's will for creation, be relevant to the events and circumstances at hand, be appropriate to the ethical concepts warranted by other symbols and experiences of the religious community, and be able to withstand the critical scrutiny of others involved in the same kinds of activities in question.[67]

The third way in which belief in God, mediated through a community, affects moral discernment and action is through the relation of religious beliefs to moral principles and values. This involves the various means by which "religious" reasons for particular courses of action are joined to or distinguished from "moral" reasons or justifications that draw acknowledgment and assent from all reasonable persons.[68] As Gustafson points out, two theoretical extremes can be demonstrated in Christian ethics: One extreme is that Christian principles are always defensible on rational grounds; the other, that Christian principles are only intelligible to followers of Jesus.[69] He sees a middle course:

> The moral act is qualified by the religious significance it has for
> the agent in the light of his or her reasons for being moral without

collapsing the two references of "good." It is a good act for two distinctive but "overlapping" reasons; it is a morally right or good act because of its consequences or because of the immediate moral principles that governed it. It is also a "good" act for the moral ultimate "theological" or "religious" reasons it was done; it was done in fidelity to God, or done to honor God.[70]

Thus, for Gustafson, belief in God is significant in individual and communal moral life in at least three ways. First, through the believer's experience of God or of senses of God, his or her dispositions, attitudes, and integrity—in short, character—are informed and transformed, and impulses of a moral order result. Second, by the articulation of human experiences through religious symbols and expressions of belief, the believer is able to make moral sense of his or her experience in relating it by analogy to the perceived activity of God in history. Religious symbols also help to disclose moral elements of our experience that might otherwise go undisclosed. Finally, in determining the reasons for moral action, believers can look not only to reasons that would hold for all rational persons, but also to "reasons" derived from a particular expression of their religious belief. The reasons for "good" actions overlap, but they may well be grounded in fidelity to, or honor of, God.

Although there is much in Gustafson's theological ethics which acknowledges a God who is active in the human realm, he refrains from delineating who that God is and how that God is present to human persons. While Gustafson asserts that the basis of human morality is interaction, and that this interaction is a medium through which God is communicated, he does not assert that God's action may be directly known in the dynamics of that human interaction. In his later work, Gustafson clearly and forcefully contends that although God is present in the interdependence of the universe, humanity may not presume that God is particularly active or, for that matter, particularly interested, in human interactions. Human beings seek the presence and affirmation of God in their interactions, but attempting to contrive God's special attention, delight, or censure in those interactions is the height of anthropocentrism.

The negation of God's special attention to humans is an unsettling thesis. Gustafson carefully presents it and its application to practical moral reasoning in his two-volume work, *Ethics from a Theocentric Perspective*, which has stirred much controversy among theological ethicists since its publication. Theocentric ethics is Gustafson's re-

sponse to the predominant strains of thought in theological ethics
and more basically, to the utilitarian view of religion as an instrument
of humanity:

> My contention is that in our own time, as much as in any other,
> religion is propagated for its utility value to individuals and com-
> munities. . . . Both individual pieties and social pieties become
> instrumental not to gratitude to God, the honor of God, or service
> of God, but to sustaining purposes to which the Deity is inciden-
> tal, if not something of an encumbrance.[71]

The result of such instrumentality is that humans lose a rightful sense
of finitude and the perspective that accurately orders relationships
and institutions.[72] According to Gustafson, this narrowing of perspective has affected the shape and content of ethics, as humans seek to
justify their actions as "moral" actions which are divinely sanctioned.
Gustafson terms this objectionable justification in which human
beings are at the core of theological ethics "anthropocentric" ethics.

Gustafson acknowledges that humans can only rely on limited
powers of perception to find the hand of God in their world, and that
theology must attend to that reality. Moreover, the interactional character of human life is dignified once again as the locus of the activity
of God, and the construction of a theological ethics is dependent on
experience:

> Human experience is prior to reflection. . . . Religion and morality
> are aspects of human experience. . . . Indeed, there is no way in
> which a certain kind of anthropocentrism can be avoided. If there
> is knowledge of God it is human knowledge of God; it is knowl-
> edge of God mediated through human experiences, either of
> one's own, of a community in which one participates, or of
> another person. . . . Neither theology nor ethics has fulfilled its
> intellectual purpose if it merely describes religious and moral
> experience, or religious and moral dimensions of aspects of expe-
> rience.[73]

Further, the human experience in which God acts and from which
theological ethics is derived is multivalent and not entirely deci-
phered in rational terms. Experience is a unity of affective, intellectual,
rational, and aesthetic elements, and therefore,

Morality as an aspect of human experience might not be as neatly divisible into aspects of the person as some moral theorists hold. . . . In morality and religion there are affective as well as cognitive and volitional aspects of experience . . . . in the rawest moments of moral concern these aspects of the self are commingled.[74]

Given the locus of God in human experience, the believer detects the movement and activity of God by analogically extrapolating from the experience of interaction with another person:

There are many who respond to another "dimension" in their affective lives and in their dispositions who do not name "gods" or "God." But for those who are identified with particular communities, the step is overt, acknowledged, and articulated in the symbols and concepts that construe the world of experience theologically and religiously. The step of monotheism is distinctive. From the experience of others or of otherness it, for reasons of heart and mind, respects and reveres *an* Other; it acknowledges dependence upon and expresses gratitude to *an* Other; it develops a sense of obligation to *an* Other, and a sense of repentance in the face of its failure to relate properly to *the* Other.[75]

What are we to make of this divine presence in human interactions? May we draw a conclusion of divine determinism from it? Gustafson answers a resounding No. For Gustafson, the presence of God in human interactions demonstrates a continuity of humanity with the rest of nature—an interdependence—and in no way denies "the import of our capacities for agency."[76] But it does affirm the appropriateness of an interactive or response-oriented model of moral action for humanity.

Gustafson distinguishes his version of this response-oriented model from that of his mentor, H. Richard Niebuhr. Niebuhr, influenced by George Herbert Mead and Martin Buber, was able to see God's action in all human actions. But Gustafson contrasts his view with Niebuhr's:

He had more confidence in the agency model of God than I have. In distinction from that view, I believe we can appropriately say only that we have capacities to respond to persons and events in an interactive way, and that through those actions we respond to the divine governance, to the powers that bear down on us and sustain us. We have capacities to discern in particular events and relations something of what the divine governance requires, what our appropriate actions and relations are to nature, to other persons, and so forth.[77]

Discernment is a central element in Gustafson's theocentric ethics, as it was in his earlier thought. Such discernment is an effort to interpret divine governance in historical circumstances and to respond to God's enabling and requiring, rather than an effort to adjust our actions to a "changeless moral order," as a natural law tradition would prescribe.[78] According to Gustafson, what can be discerned in such a scheme are the "necessary conditions for life to be sustained and developed."[79] As far as a criterion for moral action, he submits that these "necessary conditions"

are not a sufficient basis for ethics; specific ends and moral principles are not simply deduced from them. But they are a necessary basis for ethics. . . . To relate things in a manner appropriate to their relations to God requires that these patterns and processes be perceived and conceptualized as accurately as possible, and that their conditions be met.[80]

Gustafson admits that "ethics in the theocentric perspective . . . does not provide absolute moral certainty or eliminate tragedy."[81] It does, however, point our discernment in a certain direction: We become "participants" in a discernment process in which we relate to things, as parts to a whole, in a manner appropriate to their relations to God.[82] That is, we are part of a relationship of things to people, people to people, all in the context of belief in God.

In sum, the contributions of theocentric ethics to our discussion of Gustafson's notion of the role of religious belief in the moral life are limited but important. First, theocentric ethics confirms that God is the locus of theological ethics. Even if we conceive of the moral life as vitally concerned with the salvation of persons (and therefore to a certain degree anthropocentric), theocentric ethics reminds us of the fundamental truth that God is the ultimate referent for any ethics. Second, in its embrace of the theological importance of history, circumstance, and particular events, theocentric ethics promotes the idea that human interactions, seen in the light of religious belief, are by analogy expressions of our interactions with "the Other." That is, human interactions have theological significance beyond themselves.

Theocentric ethics confirms that participative discernment propelled by religious belief affords the moral agent more than merely a prudential course of action; it is itself a way of responding to "a prior reality," the reality of God.[83]

Beyond a general articulation of the influence of religious belief on the moral life, Gustafson addresses the specific issue of the influence of Jesus Christ on the moral lives of Christian believers. Because our project concerns moral discernment in the Christian tradition, we look to Gustafson as an important source of insight in determining the role of Jesus in shaping the morality and the discernment of those who believe in him. While Gustafson has undergone a rather significant evolution in his thought on this subject, which has recently put him at odds with other Christian ethicists, his earlier studies and proposals of the role of Christ in the moral life have been widely regarded as incisive and comprehensive. Gustafson sees Christian theologians, in the name of all Christian believers, pursuing the question, What ought I do? Belief is difficult to explicate, and those who assent to belief in Jesus ultimately articulate their allegiance in different forms. In *Christ and the Moral Life*, Gustafson recognizes this divergence, and formulates a model of headings under which these approaches to belief in Christ and their representative theologians may be discussed. The headings include "Jesus Christ, Lord Who is Creator and Redeemer" (Barth); "Jesus Christ the Sanctifier" (Wesley, Schleiermacher, Augustine, and Aquinas); "Jesus Christ the Justifier" (Luther, Bultmann, and Reinhold Niebuhr); "Christ the Pattern" (Bonhoeffer, Kirkegaard, and Thomas Kempis); and "Christ the Teacher" (Rauschenbusch and Ramsey).

Over and above the interactional form of the moral life and the appropriate theocentric perspective with which one approaches theological ethics, Gustafson presumes the above typologies and constructs a proposal concerning the differences that Christ does make, can make, and ought to make in the lives of Christian believers and their communities.[84] First, Christ makes a difference in the perspective and posture of the Christian. Through Jesus, one can see the possibility, the hope, the power of goodness, and one can come to trust God.[85] This trust permeates the perspective of the moral agent and allows him or her to act with confidence in the face of opposition. Second, Christ also makes a difference in the dispositions—the manner of life, habits, virtues, and "readiness to act in a certain way"—of the believer.[86] How this differs from the perspective and posture is not altogether clear, except that there is the suggestion by Gustafson that these are enduring qualities in the life of the agent, rather than passing points of view.[87]

Third, Christ informs the intentions of the disciple, thus affecting the future-orientation of the moral life of the agent. The basic task of the disciple is then to determine which of the intentions of the agent are consistent with faith in Christ.[88] "Faith" is a broad term presumed to contain many elements of the above discussions, but the most important feature of this influence is that Christ should provide a reference for future moral action. Fourth, and finally, Gustafson sees that Jesus Christ makes a difference in the believing moral agent in that Christ provides actual norms for behavior. For Gustafson, this means that Christ shows and symbolizes what God wills, that he shows what trust in God can do, and that Christ can provide particular norms for one's words and deeds.[89] Lest these ideas be interpreted too literally, Gustafson is quick to point out that Christ cannot be the only norm for Christian action and that the believer must incorporate Christ analogically, by parable and by reference to the love command.[90]

In explanation of the difference that Christ makes to the Christian believer in norms for the moral life, Gustafson mentions that Christ serves as a "source of illumination."[91] Indeed, in all of Gustafson's constructive proposals, Christ serves much the same moral function. In all cases, whether Christ affects perspective and posture, dispositions, intentions or norms for behavior, Christ principally reveals God in these different aspects of morality and thereby evokes or educes a difference in the moral life of the believing agent. This Christology is borne out in Gustafson's other writings. In delineating the distinctiveness of Christian morality, he states:

> What distinguishes the morality of the Christian community is the root and ground of its moral faith, its allegiance to Christ as the One who has come to *disclose to all* men that the Ground and Giver of life is good. . . . Christian morality is a trust in the goodness and power of God, the creator and orderer and redeemer of life; a goodness *made known* in the advent, the birth, the words and deeds, the death and new life of Jesus Christ. . . . Apart from belief, apart from assertions that *point to God through Jesus his Son*, we would not see as clearly as we do that God is worthy of our trust.[92]

Gustafson finally makes this explicit in *Ethics from a Theocentric Perspective*. His notion of Jesus' role in the moral life is ultimately one of exemplification and illumination:

> In relating ourselves and all things in a manner appropriate to their relations to God, Christians [should] be ready voluntarily to deny their own individual and collective interests for the sake of the well-being of other persons, communities and even of the natural world. This obligation is also borne out by general human experience. For Christians, however, this claim is very strong, for in the person and accounts of Jesus, who marks the particular historic identity of this community, there are poignant exemplifications in his life, activity, teaching, and death of what theocentric piety and fidelity call upon us to do.[93]

None of the facets of Gustafson's proposal contain any evidence of Christ's divine power or authority, by the action of the Holy Spirit, to transform the moral life of the individual. Herein, he parts company with many Catholic moral theologians who see in Jesus Christ the entitative authority and power of God to rule the world as its Lord, to sanctify the individual, to justify a fallen creation, to initiate in human history a forthcoming paschal pattern of dying and rising, and to promulgate distinctively divine teaching. Those espousing this entitative christology promote a different conception of Christ's effect on the moral life that stresses not only Christ's illumination of God's grace and call also but his ability by the power of the Spirit to empower the believer to receive that grace and accept that call. Nevertheless, Gustafson's christology of revelation is helpful to our project.

Gustafson's Pastoral Perspective: Church, Ministry, and the Moral Life

Given the elements of Gustafson's interactional formulation of the moral life and the role of religious belief in it, one may suspect that the Church and its ministers figure prominently in Gustafson's thought since the believing community and the give-and-take of communication is the locus of God's action. However, this action is not always evident, so by collectively attending to the content and meaning of their own interactions, especially as they are illuminated by Jesus Christ, believers must discern "what God is enabling and requiring them to do." The Church, then, is a "community of moral action," the place where believers "are particularly called to interpret their existence . . . . as the location in time and space of their responsibility to God for human society and for other persons."[94] The Church takes up the call to be a community in the name of the purposes of God—creating, sustaining, restraining, and making better the quality of life. The Church seeks to be effective in three specific areas: the ethos of the culture in which it finds itself, the interpersonal relationships within it, and the institutions to which it relates.[95]

What is the role of the minister in a church conceived of as a community of moral discourse? By the very definition of membership in such a community, the minister must be convinced of the value and theological warrant of interaction as the locus for God's call to responsibility. An appropriate leadership style will necessarily be collaborative. The ministerial leader of such a community may demonstrate certain expertise in the community's moral deliberations, but he or she has no corner on the truth in certain facets of the discussion, especially those having to do with particular practical applications of moral norms:

> The interpretation of the norms is one of the media for consensus formation. . . . The points of reference within which the "expert" does his work in part define the acceptability of what he has to say. . . . The authority of the religious expert is not granted by virtue of his knowledge and ordination, and therefore neither quiet assent nor vigorous obedience is forthcoming. The leader becomes a person whose function it is *to give guidance to a consensus-forming process,* in and through which particular judgments (including his own) can be clarified and be brought to bear on the relevant points of action.[96]

The minister is one who is convinced of the intrinsic moral value of participation in discourse aimed at interpreting God's call to responsibility. He or she freely offers pastoral and theological expertise but yields in the face of expertise in areas of related concern. He is a leader in consensus-formation in the community. When the community seeks to clarify and specify its moral intentions in line with "the God . . . who wills the well-being of his creation,"

> Specification of intention is not the task of the pastor or ecclesiastical bureaucrat alone; neither of these is sufficient in wisdom and knowledge, and each is too biased to be reliable as the sole source

of determination of the particular purposes of the church. Discourse involves mutual probing, each participant with his special skills, his gifts of wisdom, his technical knowledge, his powers of persuasion, enlightening the process toward consensus about what deeds and words are worthy of the gospel, what activities are consonant with the faith, what performances are consistent with and expressive of the beliefs of the church.[97]

The portrait here is of a minister who has enough confidence in God's presence in the interaction of the community that all participants in the moral discourse will have a voice.

Implications for Pastoral Moral Discernment

The theological ethics of James Gustafson affirm some of the basic insights about morality already postulated in the social interactional proposal of Norma Haan and her associates and by John Macmurray. First, Gustafson is a true interactional moralist. The form of the moral life is the relational life, and the experiences of the relational life ground the moral life as well. We see that Gustafson's general theory of morality is constituted by initiatives and responses, actions, and interactions. Second, and as a result of this primarily interactional perspective, Gustafson sees morality as a social phenomenon. This perspective, like Haan's and Macmurray's, is a direct challenge to the "philosopher king" model of morality, wherein isolated, rational deliberation is somehow the substance of moral action, and the solutions to moral problems lie in sheer logic and deduction.

Third, for Gustafson, community is a critical locus of moral life and development. Fourth, in its own way, Gustafson's "discourse" confirms Haan's insight that dialogue, as well as a sense of moral balance between discerners, is key to good overall discernment. Fifth, Gustafson's form of the moral life affirms the multidimensional nature of morality. He states that moral reflection is a secondary activity derived from experience, and since experience is composed of rational, affective, intellectual, and aesthetic features, morality must be similarly constituted. Finally, action is a key criterion for a moral life. For Gustafson, persons are agents capable of determining purposes and developing intentions which reach fruition in the exercise of capacities and powers. Again, Gustafson affirms this element of morality asserted by both Haan and Macmurray.

In this affirmation of the theories of Haan and Macmurray, Gustafson ratifies our contention that the give-and-take of moral discernment is not at the pastoral periphery of ethics but at the center, especially of theological ethics. Gustafson advances this form of morality by introducing personal character (or style or consistency) as a feature not heretofore stressed in either Haan or Macmurray. This feature of his thought has an important implication for our theory. Until now, we have simply stated that the foundational ethic and critical method for pastoral moral discernment have to attend to the wholeness of the person, for example, the cognitive and affective dimensions. But in Gustafson's contribution to our comprehensive theory, we note that what the person brings to the pastoral encounter by way of personal traits enters into the dialogue and likewise must receive attention. Agents do not approach the discernment process as blank moral slates but as persons formed in certain ways, who may or may not be open to further formation or to transformation through dialogical discernment.

The most important contribution that James Gustafson makes to the project at hand is that he outlines the role of religious belief in interactional moral agency. The primary implication of Gustafson's theology for our thesis is that his consideration of theological as well as psychological and philosophical foundations for pastoral moral discernment broadens the horizon of the meaning of moral activity. By attending to Gustafson's principal points, we encounter another perspective from which to approach moral activity. In "relating to others in their proper relation to God," we find a critical metaethic for interactional morality that was not afforded by either the centerpiece of our theory, Haan's proposal, or Macmurray's moral philosophy.

Gustafson's theology attaches a new significance to interaction, even beyond Macmurray's God-in-history. Gustafson shows that in the interactions, dialogues, and discourses of a collective of believers, we find the possibility of God's communication and action. This insight affords a new theological base for a phenomenon that Haan and Macmurray have already established as moral. An important implication of Gustafson's insight for pastoral moral discernment is that the dialogue between the minister and the one seeking assistance in discernment is demonstrated to be not only a sound means of determining moral action but also an occasion for the development and the transformation of one's faith in a living God.

Gustafson has also shown that belief in God can be a locus of morality. A believing agent's "senses of God"—dependence, gratitude, repentance, obligation, possibility, and direction, for example—engender imitational dispositions that can be the actual root of moral development and action. In addition to the theological significance of the form of interaction as a foundational ethic for pastoral moral discernment, we also have in this feature of Gustafson's theory a theological content for morality with direct implications for determining a method of discernment. For example, a minister may come to an understanding of the governing images and senses of God in the person seeking assistance with moral discernment. Such an understanding can assist one to explore and nurture the faith-based virtues of the person, which in turn may help the person to determine and enact a course of moral action. Because these senses and images are more in the aesthetic and emotional life of the person than in the strictly rational realm, the minister does well to attend to the emotional well-being of the one seeking assistance. The affective dimension contains not only moral but religious sentiments that are important to the process of discernment.

Gustafson's constructive proposal for the role of belief in Christ in the moral life is also a helpful one for our project. Accounting for the best of the theological proposals outlined in *Christ and the Moral Life*, Gustafson suggests that Christ has influence on the perspective, posture, disposition, and intentions of the believer. Moreover, Christ serves as the actual norm for Christian believers. In this theologically nuanced position, Gustafson notes that discipleship may be the key moral category for believers to consider in determining the role of Christ in moral discernment and action.

Obviously, Gustafson shies away from an uncritical allegiance to Christ—one based, for example, on a literal or fundamentalist interpretation of scripture. Instead, he formulates a proposal in which Christ has moral influence on the life of the believer in broad and relatively undefined ways, in "perspective" and "posture," for example. Overall, this conception of the role of Christ in the moral life is particularly suitable for inclusion in pastoral moral discernment. In matters of real moral discernment, there are often no specific answers to particular questions or predicaments. Christian tradition and scripture, in and of themselves, can rarely provide a clear answer that has direct application to the issue at hand. More often, Christian tradition and scripture, as the ongoing message of Christ, influence the discerning agent through the more general avenues that Gustafson describes. These are helpful parameters for the inclusion of belief in Christ within pastoral moral discernment.

Finally, Gustafson makes explicit recommendations regarding the role of the minister in moral discernment. There are some ecclesiological difficulties in making the transition from the ideal "community of moral discourse" to the typical Roman Catholic congregation. Nonetheless, the basic model of the role of the minister as articulated by Gustafson in *The Church as Moral Decision-Maker* draws together other observations that I have made about the role of the minister in pastoral moral discernment and could well serve as a guide for the minister in the "critical method" for pastoral moral discernment which I will construct in the last chapter. Gustafson sees the minister functioning as a guide for consensus formation, as an active participant in moral discourse who has an expertise that he or she must share but also enough confidence in the possibility of God's abiding presence in the interactions of a community of belief to yield to the positions of others in the dialogue. Such a stance, of course, runs directly counter to a more typically didactic and authoritarian model of pastoral moral discernment which is often present in many Catholic congregations.[98] Given our aim of constructing an interactive alternative to the didactic model, Gustafson's assertion of a participative, dialogical role for the minister in moral discernment is a valuable formulation for the construction of a critical method for pastoral moral discernment in the Roman Catholic tradition.[99]

NOTES

1. John Macmurray, *The Self as Agent* (London: Faber and Faber Limited, 1957), 19–20.
2. Macmurray, *Freedom in the Modern World* (London: Faber and Faber Limited, 1932), 24.
3. Macmurray, *The Self as Agent*, 27.
4. Ibid., 38.
5. Ibid., 29.
6. Ibid., 89–90.
7. Ibid., 15.
8. Macmurray, *The Self as Agent*, 187.
9. Macmurray, *Persons in Relation*, 185.

10.   Ibid., 159. See the discussion that follows on "Moral Anthropology" for an explanation of the universality of the human need for relationship and its forms. The "community" to which we refer here is Macmurray's community of "heterocentric" persons who are motivated by love of another, not those who are motivated by fear.

11.   Macmurray, *The Self as Agent,* 221–222.

12.   Macmurray, *The Structure of Religious Experience,* 17.

13.   Ibid.

14.   Ibid., 72–73.

15.   John Macmurray, *Reason and Emotion* 2nd ed. (London: Faber and Faber Limited, 1961), 238.

16.   Ibid., 249.

17.   Macmurray, *The Self as Agent,* 34–37.

18.   In this discussion and in later ones, I refer to Macmurray's own scheme, which is posed in terms of a "mother" as the primary caregiver and a male child. My use of female and male pronouns follows Macmurray's pattern.

19.   Macmurray, *Persons in Relation,* 44–63.

20.   Macmurray, *The Self as Agent,* 38.

21.   Macmurray, *Persons in Relation,* 22.

22.   Macmurray, *The Self as Agent,* 89.

23.   Ibid., 130.

24.   See Macmurray, *Persons in Relation,* 99–104.

25.   Ibid., 105.

26.   Macmurray, *Freedom in the Modern World,* 58.

27.   John Macmurray, *Conditions of Freedom* (London: Faber and Faber Limited, 1949), 27.

28.   Macmurray, *Freedom in the Modern World,* 64.

29.   Macmurray, *Persons in Relation,* 27.

30.   Macmurray, *Reason and Emotion,* 5.

31.   Macmurray, *Persons in Relation,* 33.

32.   Macmurray, *Reason and Emotion,* 20.

33.   Ibid., 23, 30.

34.   Ibid., 18.

35.   Macmurray, *Freedom in the Modern World,* 55.

36.   Macmurray, *Reason and Emotion,* 39.

37.   Ibid., 60.

38.   Macmurray, *Reason and Emotion,* 125.

39.   Ibid., 123–124.

40.   Macmurray, *Persons in Relation,* 158.

41.   Ibid., 163–165.

42.   James M. Gustafson, *Can Ethics Be Christian?* (Chicago: University of Chicago Press, 1975), 13–14.

43.   Gustafson is careful to point out that these assertions do not constitute *a* pattern or *the* pattern of the moral life. They are instead "generalizations about the fundamental conditions necessary for moral judgments, moral decisions and moral actions to occur." (Ibid., 14.)

44. Gustafson, *Can Ethics Be Christian?*, 15–19.
45. Gustafson, *Theology and Christian Ethics* (Philadelphia: Pilgrim Press, 1974), 100–101.
46. Ibid., 102–105.
47. Ibid., 106.
48. Ibid., 106–108.
49. Gustafson, *Theology and Christian Ethics*, 39ff.
50. Ibid., 44.
51. Gustafson, *Can Ethics Be Christian?*, 28.
52. Ibid., 25–28.
53. Ibid., 31.
54. Ibid., 46.
55. Ibid., 47.
56. Ibid., 29.
57. Gustafson, *Theology and Christian Ethics*, 42.
58. Ibid., 117.
59. Gustafson, *Can Ethics Be Christian?*, 156–157.
60. Ibid., 86.
61. See Ibid., 87–91.
62. Ibid., 92–94.
63. Ibid., 118–120.
64. Ibid., 132–142.
65. Ibid., 123.
66. Ibid., 128–129.
67. Ibid., 142–143.
68. Ibid., 145–146.
69. Ibid., 167.
70. Ibid., 174.
71. James M. Gustafson, *Ethics from a Theocentric Perspective,* Volume One (Chicago: University of Chicago Press, 1981), 18.
72. Ibid., 20.
73. Ibid., 115.
74. Ibid., 118–119.
75. Ibid., 135–136.
76. Ibid., 273.
77. Ibid., 274.
78. Ibid., 338.
79. Ibid., 339.
80. Ibid., Volume 2, 298.
81. Ibid., Volume 1, 342.
82. Ibid., Volumes 2, 13, and 16.
83. Ibid., 13.
84. James M. Gustafson, *Christ and the Moral Life*, 240.
85. Ibid., 243–247.
86. Ibid., 248–249.
87. Ibid., 248.

88. Ibid., 261.

89. Ibid., 265.

90. Ibid., 268–269.

91. Ibid., 266.

92. Gustafson, *Theology and Christian Ethics*, 55–56 (emphases added).

93. Gustafson, *Ethics from a Theocentric Perspective*, Volume 2, 319.

94. James M. Gustafson, *The Church as Moral Decision-Maker* (Philadelphia: Pilgrim Press, 1970), 71.

95. Ibid., 66–70.

96. Gustafson, *The Church as Moral Decision-Maker*, 130–131.

97. Ibid., 154.

98. In minimizing the hierarchical role, Gustafson parallels Avery Dulles's ecclesiological type of "servant," which stresses the ministerial empowerment of all the baptized, as well as the "mystical communion" type, which stresses the communal aspects of the church. (See Avery Dulles, *Models of the Church* [Garden City, NY: Doubleday and Company, 1974], especially 43–57 and 83–96.) As will become more evident in ensuing chapters, I favor these types for the purpose at hand, though both types carry attendant criticisms. Nonetheless, I believe they contribute much to the description of contemporary pastoral responsibilities, notably an ethic and method for pastoral moral discernment.

99. Ibid., 159.

5

A CONVERSATION AMONG THE INTERACTIONAL THEORIES: Toward a Foundational Ethic for Pastoral Moral Discernment

In this chapter we will relate the theories of Haan, Macmurray, and Gustafson to each other to form a relational foundational ethic for pastoral moral discernment. The development of a relational ethic allows for the articulation of formal values that can serve as guidelines for pastoral moral discernment, especially in the Roman Catholic tradition, which currently suffers a lacuna in its theory about the pastoral translation of moral teachings.

Among Haan, Macmurray, and Gustafson we detect common thematic features. We will concentrate on five features under which we will subsume the conversations between them: the role of human history; a multidimensional view of the human person; the use of subjective imagination and creativity in forging solutions to moral problems; the relational and communal nature of morality; and the role of belief in God and Jesus Christ in moral agency and action. In the course of the conversations according to these themes, we will begin to provide the actual elements of a foundational Christian ethic that will not only guide pastoral moral discernment in the Catholic tradition but also offer the contours of a critical method for that discernment.

I. An Ethic Grounded in History

The admission of history as a basis for a Christian ethic is perhaps the most important and comprehensive methodological shift in Catholic moral reflection in recent time. Because it has been largely synonymous with a nonhistorical interpretation of the natural law tradition, Catholic thought has been dominated by the application of unchanging moral principles to virtually all of life's contingencies. Such pastoral practice has in the main minimized the role of the individual person in decision making, downplayed of the subjective element in discernment, and evidenced a paralyzing conservatism in which particular contexts and situations were dismissed as mere accidents in an otherwise predetermined objective moral order to which all people must submit. In short, time was merely the medium through which the objective order played itself out; because change and development were only accidental, they assumed little importance as moral categories and required no interpretation.

With the admission of history as a base for Christian ethics, the human experiences of change and development assume a new significance. Time becomes the ongoing chronicle of God's salvation of humanity, and therefore discrete events are not accidents but express the substance of God's gratuitous love. Individual events in time require interpretation as the unfolding of God's creative plan. Persons are not cogs in a well-oiled machine, but agents of change and development—co-creators whose experiences are worthy gauges of the ways in which God acts.

According to Norma Haan, moral development and action are conceived in the experiences of everyday life. Morality for Haan is not a speculative matter, but a practical, experiential one. By attending to the ways in which we actually seek and achieve moral balances in our everyday lives, we come to know the answer to the question, "What is morality?" Because morality is constituted in the process and the outcome of a dialogical interchange, we can note with assurance that action in a given circumstance, "is regarded, in everyday life, as the only authentic criterion of moral truth."[1] Action, a pivotal consideration bounded in time by an observable beginning, middle, and end, reflects a historical consciousness in Haan's theory of morality. Moreover, Haan asserts that one's growth in the course of new and repeated actions and situations constitutes moral development. In even proposing the idea of the moral development of the person, she accedes to the concept of change in the moral order. Haan may even be criticized for her rather radically situational conception of morality. Joining the social learning theorists of morality, she is most skeptical of the notion of "character," or some fixed constellation of moral qualities in the agent which perdures over time.

All of this demonstrates Haan's grounding of morality in time and experience. As an empiricist, she points to the exigencies and dynamics of everyday living to yield a theory of morality. As a result, Haan can serve as the cornerstone of our foundational ethic. As Catholic moral theology moves away from the classicist world view to a recognition of history and toward an appreciation of action, situation, and praxis as determinants of morality, empiricists such as Haan offer an adequate understanding of the moral life in general and pastoral moral discernment in particular.

Macmurray shares Haan's predisposition for action-in-history as the principal criterion for morality. Macmurray's work is devoted to establishing the basic anthropological position of humanity as "I do," over and against the predominant strains of critical philosophy, in which "I think" is the starting point for moral reflection. As Macmurray seeks to construct a "form of the personal" in which the human relationship is the basis for morality, he sees the "I think" position as overly rationalized, abstract, isolationist, and outside the realm of historical existence. Recall Macmurray's case against the adequacy of the "I think" position:

> If we start with the solitary individual, self-isolated in reflection, and consider him existing as a thinker, we do exclude the normal sources of error, and his existence becomes an ideal existence. . . . So we all rise above the sources of error, which lie in the limitation of a spatio-temporal existence and the practical necessities it imposes; above bias and prejudice; above the particularities of circumstance and experience which account for our differences from one another. So we all enter a logical heaven, where there is nothing to sully the pure exercise of reason, and to think is to think the truth.[2]

While Macmurray shares this practical, action-oriented, historical grounding with Haan, he extends his effect by actually introducing the significance of history. Beginning with the assertion of the "I do" position, he states that we may conceive of the history of the world as the intentional action of agents, rather than as accidents occurring to subjects. If one assents to such a conception, one can also imagine that the history of the world is really one action, the intentional action of one Agent, God.[3] Such a move is not made facilely, and for a person to imagine such a singularly intended personal universe is no less than to make an important act of faith. Nonetheless, Macmurray states that for religious persons, the world cannot be seen differently. In faith, the believer sees the universe, constituted in all of its circumstances, eventualities, particularities, limits of time and space, as the "field" of God's personal and intentional action. As such, the field of religious experience is coterminous with everyday experience, history gains significance as the domain of God's purposes, and a human morality that attends to the dynamics of history is valid and true for the believer.

Macmurray's overall thesis regarding the significance of history augments and complements Haan's position. While believers can learn much from Haan's parameters of actual moral functioning and development, Macmurray lends greater significance to the everyday interactions that are morality for Haan. Through Macmurray's work, we come to see that the particular situations of people have an even deeper significance than they do in Haan's true theory of morality. Indeed, we may have in Macmurray's historically based theory, a "best" theory of morality.

Gustafson provides additional impetus to attend to the exigencies of human history. Gustafson's methodology is "theologically empirical." He begins with human experience, interprets it, and draws normative assumptions from it. Like both Haan and Macmurray, Gustafson sees the moral life as culminating in action. In such a view, persons are agents capable of intentional action, not merely subjects of the forms of a static universe. This view reveals an importance for history and for individual events.

> As agents, they have the capacities to determine themselves to some extent; they can intend to exercise their capacities in certain ways and can follow through on such intention. . . . Persons are not merely passive chips floating on rivers of events and circumstances and carried by whatever currents flow. Rather, they are agents or actors.[4]

Instead of basing belief in God as Macmurray does on a single Agent with a single, personal intention for the universe, Gustafson asserts that a person can come to belief analogically through experiences with an other such that an Other is discovered.[5] He asserts the importance of history as a base for ethics by showing that the believer detects in everyday experiences more than the vicissitudes of human interactions. A believer looks to events and interactions because God is present in history.

> The horizon of [the believer's] vision, both of his responsibilities and of his aspirations, extends beyond the time and space box in which he fixes his moral action for reasons of practical necessity to a power which renders new possibilities and new hopes. His involved discernment is not only in finding what is right and good in the circumstances in which he acts, but in seeking what God is requiring and making possible.[6]

Gustafson, like Macmurray, deepens the significance of Haan's proposal by stating that in the case of the believer, one uses historical circumstances as grist for the mill of theological reflection, as the very stuff of God's being-in-the-world. Historical events are more than mere events, and interaction is more than interaction. So for Haan, the empirical inquiry into the nature of everyday morality helps us discover what morality is. For Gustafson, the findings of that study reveal more than simply knowledge about morality. They reveal "responsibilities and aspirations which extend beyond the time and space box . . . to a power which renders new possibilities and new hopes." The world of events, circumstances, and interactions—the world of human history—is not only interesting but theologically meaningful.

A synthesis of the perspectives of the three interactionists on the role of history and historical method that helps to establish our foundational ethic can be stated as follows: *The ethic is based on the phenomena of changing human experiences and the articulation of them as discrete historical events that we may interpret and to which we attach theological significance.*

II. A Multivalent Moral Anthropology

Turning our attention to moral agency, we now compare the views of the human person and how they affect moral decision making, action, and development. For each of the interactional theorists, we look at the fundamental moral anthropology, the perspectives on moral motivation, the roles of personal cognition and emotion in the moral life, and the incorporation of character.

Haan has a positive view of the human person, who, from the time of earliest development, tends toward reciprocity, being good, and doing the right thing in conjunction with others. Unlike the psychoanalytic perspective, for example, in which the moral life is a

mediation within the ego of basically selfish impulses toward plea-
sure, and unlike the social learning perspective, which stresses value
neutrality in the earliest stages of life, Haan proposes that the newborn is "morally naive, but immediately induced to participate recip-
rocally." Unlike the Freudian conception, in which the unsuccessful
resolution of the Oedipal complex results in a fairly determined (and
somewhat mysterious) deficiency in moral functioning for the dura-
tion of one's life, Haan sees moral development as depending on the
quality of social interchange and the successful resolution of actual
situations. The positive implication of Haan's view is that mistakes
in moral judgment and performance may be committed and assimilated for the agent's future reference, but these defaults are not indicative of a fundamental egocentricity or value neutrality. The impulse toward reciprocity, cooperation, and equalization with others
endures. Haan avers a natural reciprocity that serves as a motiva-
tional factor in moral decision making and action. Both positive and
negative motivations flow from this basic desire for reciprocity:

> Moral motivation has both a negative and positive thrust; the
> human network of interdependency makes it so. Its negative
> push is the threat of disrupted relationships; its positive pull is
> toward enhanced relationships.[7]

If her explanation for moral motivation seems inordinately simple,
Haan adds that "people commit themselves to this moral interdepen-
dency for more private motivations":

> They have compelling needs to regard themselves as moral; they
> need to participate in order to protect their legitimate self-inter-
> ests; and they want to live in a morally predictable world.[8]

Moral motivation is a composite of genuine, strong, and natural impulses toward reciprocity as well as motivations of personal image,
protection of self-interests, and the comfort of a morally predictable
world.

Other "private" motivations can undermine the dialogue, as
shown in Haan's extended thesis of "coping and defending," a study
of how agents enter or block dialogue, depending on their motivation. Agents are motivated either to reach equalization between parties or positions, or fearfully to defend their own individual welfare in
the forms of image, self-interest, or predictability. The roles of such

fear and defensiveness, and the personal affective satisfaction of actually reaching a balanced and apt solution to a given moral problem,
suggest that a critical part is played by emotions in the moral life
according to the interactional proposal:

> The words for the reactions that follow the obstruction of moral
> motivations are all emotion words: outrage, indignation, dis-
> grace, shame, umbrage, taken-in, cheated, belittled, ripped-off,
> and so forth. And they follow not just the obstruction of moral
> motivation; even the threat of obstruction is sufficient. On the
> other side of the coin, consummation of people's moral motiva-
> tions produces the glow of the good conscience and in groups, a
> sense of well-being and camaraderie that their moral viability is
> affirmed. Thus, it seems moral action must be explained in terms
> of emotion as well as cognition.[9]

The interactional experiments yield important findings regarding
the notion of "character," or a relatively fixed constellation of moral
qualities of the person that transcend the demands of a specific situation. Haan's extensive research tends to show that participants in the
experiments who tested at a certain level in Kohlberg's scheme[10] did
not maintain a characteristic moral functioning in the interactive situations,[11] but only in very restricted settings:

> [The] results suggest that some consistency in moral character
> occurs when situations are similar, dilemmas are hypothetical,
> and interpersonal relations are equable. Real life seldom provides
> such a series of bland moral dilemmas.[12]

For Haan, persons may exhibit characteristic ways of facing moral
dilemmas, but even these are situationally relative in that different
coping and defending ego processes are employed by the person
according to such factors as the emotional distance of the person from
the situation and whether the group process of discernment was led
or dominated. Prescinding from these "characteristic" ways of functioning, the interactional proposal for morality seems to negate the
common wisdom that moral agency is a matter of drawing upon fixed
personal qualities. Instead, the moral anthropology of the interactional proposal depicts a person with a whole range of practiced dialogical skills that are then employed in creative, inductive ways in
response to the demands of a situation. This range of skills is the only
characteristic behavior Haan found. In a significant number of cases,

the mode of dialogue was the preferred and cherished mode of problem solving when situations were optimal and participants could "cope."[13]

Macmurray's articulation of the human condition is much akin to Haan's. As an empiricist, Haan is disinclined to use the terms "nature" or "natural" in her description of the human condition. Macmurray, consciously moving away from a natural law tradition in his work, nevertheless alludes to a very positive "nature" of humans in his theory of morality. Everything has a nature, and when a given thing or person expresses its nature in action, it is free. Without entering the thicket of actually describing human nature, Macmurray does describe what human freedom is—the freedom to apprehend and enjoy a world outside ourselves and live in communion with others who do the same.[14] This positive freedom to apprehend and enjoy a world outside ourselves in company with others is a basic feature of humanity. Macmurray's view of humanity is hopeful, and his morality reflects that hope.

Based on her own observation and testing, Haan describes a fundamental reciprocity in the person. Macmurray seems to consult psychology of some kind to make an identical claim in his "mother and child" thesis, but no mention of a psychology is made. Instead, as with any philosophical anthropology, to substantiate the claim we have only Macmurray's clear thinking and good word that such is the way things are. His theory is that moral motivation results from the resolution of the conflict in the child resulting from the inevitable withdrawal of constant care and attention of the mother in early childhood. Successful resolution results in an interdependence, a genuine love for the mother, which endures for the rest of life as the basis of intentions for action and moral motivation. Aborted resolution of the conflict leads to a fear-based extortion of affection from the mother, either by passive "fleeing" or by aggressive "fighting." In short, genuinely interdependent love and defensive fears of isolation are the two basic motives for action. The former engenders moral action; the latter obstructs moral action.

Regardless of the disparity in how Macmurray and Haan arrive at their positions regarding the basic view of the human condition and the basis for moral motivation, the similarities are striking. Both theorists speak of a natural reciprocity in the human person that tends toward communion with others and away from the disruption of relationships. Additionally, for Haan, "private" motivations allow one to maintain a view of the self as moral, protect self-interest and gain comfort in a predictable moral universe. Macmurray shares with Haan the idea that when the self and its needs are not regarded, defensiveness rooted in fear occurs and undermines moral action. For Macmurray, this defensiveness is played out in fleeing or fighting. Haan specifies the defensiveness as the "defending" forms of the ego processes which are also "coping" mechanisms for establishing real moral balances of reciprocity. Reciprocal, heterocentric love and isolationist, egocentric fear are the positive and negative motivations for morality. Macmurray, like Haan, admits a central role for the emotions in the moral life. But while Haan's theory of the role of emotions in moral decision making and action revolves around her coping and defending thesis, Macmurray's thesis regarding the emotions is borne out of his "I and You" position, the corrective to the "I think" position that would acclaim rationalistic and individualistic thought as the locus of moral life. This "I and You" position gives us a window to Macmurray's view of the emotions. Macmurray makes a case for "emotional reason," a concept that defers to a human capacity for reflection that is subjective and objective, evaluative and logical. According to Macmurray, we must place our values in dialogue with others so that we may confirm our own reflections against the perceptions of others' emotional reason. But for Macmurray more than for Haan, emotions and the nonrational "senses" of things are what give us the capacity to evaluate in the first place:

> Our dilemma lies in the fact that we cannot decide what would be the best to do because we cannot decide what is best worth having. That is a dilemma, not between the heart and the head, but in the heart. What is worthwhile cannot be decided by thinking, by intellect, by science, but only by emotion.[15]

Macmurray does have a relatively minor theory of "character," which is related to moral motivation:

> All action contains necessarily an element of reaction to stimulus, without which it would be impossible. We call this habit; and the system of habits in an individual agent we call character.[16]

For Macmurray, habits are not merely organic responses to stimuli; they are learned. Although they are subject to reform and modification and may be complicated by cognition, they are considered actions which have motives.[17] Insofar as they are part of a response to a stimulus that is also intentional, habits are aspects of intentional activity and experience, and thus a part of moral action. Therefore, character as the system of habits present in a person is invoked as a moral theme principally in looking to one's past action and attempting a prediction for the future. But the effect of a specific intention by which one would stray from one's character in a given situation is not discounted.[18]

> We must not forget, however, that the patterns of feeling which constitute our motives are themselves the product of an intentional experience; and that they continue responses to the environment which have been deliberately established in the past. The impulsive activities of an agent are therefore normally "in character;" though they are not determined by the present intention. A person's character is the persistent system of motives from which he acts under normal conditions; and when we predict what he is likely to do in given conditions from a knowledge of his character, we abstract from intention, and suppose that his motives will determine his actions.[19]

To Haan, for whom "characteristic action" is the only observable and reportable phenomenon, Macmurray's theory may seem illusory in its claims. But Macmurray's definition of "character" takes into account its elusive quality of simultaneously existing as an intentional and unintentional force in the moral life.

While Gustafson does not have a distinct and systematic description of his "fundamental view of humanity," several important features of such a view are evident in his work. Basic to his view is the contention that all of life is interdependent before God, who is the "power that bears down upon us." Notably, humans do not enjoy a privileged position in the universe, and God does not take special interest or delight in their role in the life of creation. Human persons simply share an interdependence with other creatures which God enables. But Gustafson posits a definite interactional tendency in the human person:

> I believe we can say appropriately only that we have capacities to respond to persons and events in an interactive way, and that through those actions we respond to the divine governance, to the powers that bear down on us and sustain us.[20]

In contrast to Macmurray's interdependence, which is rooted in a personal, particularistic experience of relation with the mother, Gustafson's interdependence is the basic form of human life, but it has no specific personal referent. Remarkably, Gustafson's notion more closely approximates Haan's view of humanity as fundamentally reciprocal, cooperative, and equalizing, but without a special reference as to how such reciprocity came about in human beings. God made us this way, but God made all creation this way. Similarly, basic morality will parallel the respective views of humanity. For Haan, morality consists of the actual ways and means of equalizing with other reciprocal beings. For Macmurray, it is the radical human freedom to be heterocentric in company with others. And for Gustafson, the position of the human person is relativized in the larger scheme of things, such that morality consists of relating things in a manner appropriate to their relations to God rather than ourselves. Morality is theocentric and no longer anthropocentric.

Gustafson's theory of moral motivation flows from the basic relational form of the moral life. Like Haan and Macmurray, motivation comes from the maintenance and enhancement of relationships. It also flows from theocentricity and is understandably rooted beyond the relationships themselves, in God. While many have noted a discontinuity between Gustafson's earlier and later work, some detectable consistency exists between this view of humanity and Gustafson's more widely acclaimed theory of the senses of God, which forms his basic scheme of moral motivation. Senses of God, such as dependence, gratitude, repentance, obligation, possibility, and direction, are realized in our interactions with others.

Gustafson constructs an explanation of the roots of moral motivation as follows: As we have known God to be for us in a certain way, so we are for others in that same way. Because God is at the center of moral motivation, we are disposed to act in a certain way. The senses of God imply a personal God who has more interest in us than Gustafson's theocentric ethics would suggest. Nonetheless, we can at least say that there is a consistency in the God-centeredness of moral motivation. This assertion would also hold for Gustafson's other moral motivators, including religious symbols, principles, and values. Christ may be considered in the same light, as a revealer of God as the center of value. Christ motivates us by illuminating a way of life in which all things are ordered according to their relationship to God.

Finally, in regard to moral motivation, while Gustafson does see the importance of relationship, in comparison to Macmurray, he is relatively silent on the moral motivation of love. Moreover, Gustaf-

son, unlike Macmurray and Haan, does not say much about the negative moral motivation of defensive fear.

Gustafson would agree with Haan and Macmurray that affective
factors play a critical role in the moral life. To locate so much of the
moral life in the world of "sense," "disposition," "interdependence,"
and "belief," for example, is to suggest that moral action is not the
strict domain of rationality, logic, and the application of principles.
Because Gustafson's moral theology is "empirical theology," a systematic reflection on experience, we would expect him to admit the
critical role of the emotions:

> Morality as an aspect of human experience might not be as neatly
> divisible into aspects of the person as some moral theorists
> hold. . . . In morality and religion there are affective as well as
> cognitive and volitional aspects of experience . . . in the rawest
> moments of moral concern these aspects of the self are com-
> mingled.[21]

Haan lists specific ego processes that assist and hinder moral
functioning; Gustafson notes specific dispositions that are morally
formational. The difference is that another person is the direct object
of the emotions for Haan, while Gustafson's senses of God involve
another person only analogically and imaginatively for the purpose of
morality. These senses are remarkably similar to Macmurray's senses,
which one must cultivate to develop emotional reason. Although
Macmurray does not center these senses in God, their importance as
the locus of evaluating the ends of things is much on a par with the
importance that Gustafson accords to his "senses." Haan and Macmurray argue the significance of emotions in their methodological
considerations of morality. Gustafson, too, incorporates the emotional life as the flourishing of the religious impulses undergirding
the moral life.

Much more than either Haan or Macmurray, Gustafson believes
in character. Gustafson does not attempt to settle whether the important question of character can be supported empirically. Haan's
answer to such a question is a qualified "no." Gustafson and Macmurray theorize about character in terms of the moral predictability of
a given person based on enduring constellations of traits which sometimes enable and sometimes obstruct sound discernment and good
moral action. While these traits do not determine the moral action of
a particular agent, Gustafson states that they are "conditions which

make possible and likely certain sorts of actions."[22] The constellations of traits are first considered by Gustafson as "consistency," "integrity," or "style," but he later makes the stronger claim that character describes "the sort of person one is."[23] This assertion is central to his theological anthropology. For Gustafson, a person is constituted not only by his or her relationships (as Macmurray and Haan believe), but also by features of personality which are relatively stable, including features over which the agent has control, such as beliefs, dispositions, and intentions, and uncontrollable features such as genetic endowment or psychiatric illness. Insofar as belief in God is part of one's character, the possibility of character as a moral category is essential to Gustafson's moral anthropology.

What might we do about the apparent disparity between Haan's minimal assent to character and Macmurray's and Gustafson's more significant assertions of its value in the moral life? We can at least note that there are some enduring features of a person's moral constitution which carry over from situation to situation, and that an agent carries to a decision or action some personal history which is brought to bear on that decision or action.

We can synthesize the perspectives of Haan, Macmurray, and Gustafson on moral anthropology with the following statements: *The human person is not merely an object in the events of life, but a free moral agent who responds to those events on a number of levels, notably, the intellectual and emotional levels. Because persons bring a relatively stable individual history to each moral action, the agent's particular responses may be "characteristic," but their actual form is open to change, renewal, and transformation.*

III. Subjectivity, Creativity, and Induction in Moral Decision Making and Action

Haan places great stock in radical subjectivity, creativity, and induction in the dialogue conducted within the consciousness of the agent, between two agents, or between an institutional entity and the agent. That dialogue is conceived as being completely open-ended. Any outcome that is determined by the "parties" is acceptable, as long as no party has subverted the full participation of any person or position. In the dialogue, parties exchange their particular dynamics and demands, and work toward either a constructive or a restorative solution of equalization. One of the principal criteria for the adequacy of the solution is that it works.[24] The appropriate use of moral principles or "the moral tradition" is characterized as "creative."[25] Because she does not define her meaning of "creative," we are left to discern its meaning as "selective," "interpretive," or as any one of a number of other synonymous definitions. But one thing is clear. The parties who forge the moral balance are bound by few if any restrictive, extrinsic demands to which they must answer, either as they commence, conduct, or terminate the dialogue. And again, Haan makes almost no room for character. It is interesting to recall the metaphor that she uses to describe the investigation of the nature of morality: rebuilding our raft at sea, plank by plank. In short, we start with little except an impulse to reach an equalized agreement.

For Haan, moral action starts from a blank-slate position, even though she resists the notion that moral agency begins there. One's imagination is stretched to envision the dialogue of persons with infinitely elastic biases of value and limited characteristic ways of resolving moral difficulties. Since Haan makes room for the role of emotions in her moral anthropology, she clearly allows for some form of emotional constitution. Emotions are not simply free-floating but come from some emotional life stability. Dialogue is a highly particularized, creative moral response to the demands of conflicting or competing positions or parties. As agents, they have the capacity to determine the outcome. But the seemingly ex nihilo creative moral response borders on the suprahuman.

In affirming the subjective, personal, reciprocal, and creative nature of morality, Macmurray characterizes, more thoroughly than Haan, the dynamics of the dialogue that leads to moral response. We can fairly add that he is able to do so because his theoretical domain, moral philosophy, allows him to make assertions about the nature of morality that are not necessarily experimentally verified. In characterizing the dialogue, he adds two important qualifications to Haan's relatively unchecked creativity in forming the solutions to moral problems.

First, Macmurray makes allowance for character, the "persistent system of motives under which [the agent] acts under normal conditions." This character is most useful in determining a qualified predictability of the agent. The agent still forms particular intentions suited to the demands at hand. But the agent does not come to the dialogue as a completely malleable consciousness. This position is an advance over Haan's thesis which, in its silence about personal constitutive values and behaviors, neglects a feature of the moral life that is, if not testable, at least intuitively affirmed. Second, Macmurray comments on the content of dialogue and specifically notes its corrective feature. If an agent employs Macmurray's "emotional reason," that by which the agent has a "sense of reality," the agent will also want to *test* his or her sense of reality, his or her personal appropriation of value, by submitting it to the critique of another.

Gustafson also sees moral decision making and action as creative, subjective, and inductive processes. In decision-making, sound discernment is required, a sufficient and accurate accounting of the reality at stake in a given situation. This discernment should culminate in fitting action. In both cases, Gustafson affirms the use of imaginative capacities. Discernment requires the ability to "see all that there is," to be "penetrating and accurate in observation" of a situation, the ability to "locate a detail," and to be "accurate in perception."[26] Discernment is thus a matter of distinguishing important from unimportant information, determining the relationships of parts to the whole, and appropriately interpreting that information. Gustafson notes that the two critical personal qualities in discernment are sensitivity and flexibility. The action, the fruit of such discernment, is also grounded in a resourcefulness that goes beyond the merely cognitive, logical, and deductive application of principles to particular situations. Borrowing a description from H. Richard Niebuhr, Gustafson calls this action "fitting" because it is tailored to the time, place, and circumstances of the situation.

The actual process leading to sound discernment and fitting action is a dialogue like that described by Haan. There is a necessary give-and-take from which the agents are able to perceive things about themselves and others. Gustafson describes what the interaction yields: imagination, possibilities, different natures of the problem at hand, interpretation, sensibilities, and empathy. Dispositions are formed, powers and limitation are made known; we gain confidence as moral actors, and we see the presence of evil.[27] The products of the process, like the process itself, are much more inductive reasoning, imagery, and creative vision than deductive reasoning, procedure, and critical analysis. Gustafson, however, does not dismiss the latter categories as unimportant. Quite the contrary, Gustafson asserts that sound discernment is a combination of the involvement of interaction with others and the disinterest of one's own critical and analytical capacities.[28]

In Gustafson's clear declaration of the importance of character, he, like Macmurray, allows for the stable values of the agents to have a deep effect on the interaction itself. Gustafson's and Macmurray's allowance for character as a content in the interaction differentiates them from Haan. For both Macmurray and Gustafson, character acts as a control of sorts, because the negotiation and the outcome of the dialogue have certain boundaries because of the relatively stable content of the agents' moral lives.

Additionally, Gustafson sees one's disposition and character as influenced, formed, and transformed by religious belief. The fitting action emerges from discernment that not only includes inductive and imaginative elements but also refers to the beliefs of the agent in the guiding question "What is God enabling and requiring in this situation?" Relying on active faith in God and the "horizon" that accompanies faith, one answers that question by looking to elements such as imagination, perception, and the authority of subjectivity as resources for discernment and action.

How Haan, Macmurray, and Gustafson concur and differ in their assertions about the qualities of moral discernment and action can be formulated in the following statement, another feature of our foundational ethic: *Consistent with the importance of history and a multivalent moral anthropology, the moral agent draws significantly on the resources of subjectivity, creativity, and induction in the process of moral discernment and in determining the course of moral action.*

IV. A Relational Ethic, A Moral Community

Haan's "thin assumptions of value" lead her to the assertion that morality is interaction. Her reluctance to describe an agent's character lies in the fact that she sees morality as that which occurs between and among agents; to concentrate on the individual traits of one agent or another is to neglect the essence of morality, the dynamic between the agents. Recall that the guiding inquiry for Haan is "What is morality?", not "What is the good?" or "What is virtue?" Framing the question in this way, she speaks of a person's action and the effect that action has on others. Departing from efforts by psychologists to de-

scribe morality in terms of the singular agent's cognitive development, satisfaction of primitive impulses, or accrual of mores from a
given culture, Haan has sought instead to study morality in practice,
the "practical, everyday morality that given the opportunity, all people would presumably endorse as the way they would ideally act."[29]
Because she focuses on the creative tension between persons in conflict and collaboration over issues of value, her task is circumscribed.
She sees the human person as naturally reciprocal. Change and
development in the moral life are contingent upon social disequilibrium between agents, not on a cognitive disequilibrium within the
agent.

Haan also insists on the full and equal participation of agents in a
given moral situation. In seeking a moral solution, participants must
articulate all positions, contributions, and expectations carefully,
openly, and fully. First, agents must commence and conduct the dialogue on an equal footing, or at least on as nearly an equal footing as
possible. Such equality requires that no one, by virtue of role or position, for example, enjoy an unchecked advantage in the dialogue. By
the same token, the environment for the exchange must encourage
agents to share their actual concerns without fear of reproach. Second, particular emotional maneuvers which block effective dialogue,
namely the defending ego processes that Haan outlines, must give
way to a real coping, which is the unguarded participation in a moral
solution. Such participative coping results in a higher level of moral
adequacy in the balances forged by the agents.[30]

It is interesting that while one may certainly detect the relational
nature of the interactional proposal, Haan offers no extended theory
of community as do Macmurray and Gustafson. In her proposal,
Haan does not explore either one's obligations to a community or
the universalizability of claims in a community.[31] Group contexts are
acknowledged as critical factors, for example, in the characterization
of friendship groups or familial backgrounds.[32] But community as a
moral entity standing on its own is not a prominent part of the interactional proposal.

Macmurray affirms relationality as the core of morality. Contrary
to Aristotle's conception of human moral development as the unfolding of potential rationality through the organic acquisition of habits
and traits, Macmurray states that the newborn is not an unfolding of
anything, but an innately relational being who is merely helpless and
in need of the care of another from the very beginning. That need of

another, the need of some dynamic relation, makes the newborn a person. Macmurray boldly asserts that, "in virtue of this fact, he is a person. . . . His *essential natural human endowment* is the impulse to communicate with another human being" (emphases added).[33]

Another approach by Macmurray to relationality in the moral life is his insistence that moral action in the world is in the "form of the personal." By the "form of the personal," Macmurray means that the agent is not an observer, but a participant in the world, not a subject looking out on events of the world, but an agent bringing about change in the world through cooperation with others. One's relation to the world is not knowing in the sense of "knowing of" or "knowing about," but knowing in the way that one knows a close friend. For Macmurray, when knowing is most free, it is "apprehending and enjoying a world outside of itself in company with others."[34] His understanding of interdependence, like Haan's interpretation of equalization, is the motivation by which various personal needs and claims are taken into account. But while Haan's equalization is ultimately founded on the respect and assimilation of the interests of both parties, Macmurray's interdependence aims at a genuine love. Haan's equalization may be undermined by defending mechanisms that abort it. Macmurray's interdependence may be undermined by manipulation through the pseudo-loves of fighting and fleeing. Despite this divergence, the similarity between Haan and Macmurray in the relational conception of the moral life is striking.

Macmurray does articulate a theory of community. Motivated by the giving and receiving of true, heterocentric, interdependent love of others, we come to know that even as we are apprehending and evaluating others, we are being apprehended and evaluated by them. Such an experience of relationality with others can lead us by extrapolation to an experience of an Other, God. By that experience, we come to know that we are creatures in a relational world, parts in a relational whole. Religion is the conscious realization of that truth, and for that reason, it is primarily constituted in the experience of community. According to Macmurray, our demand for communion is not merely a matter of respecting the interests and claims of others, as it is for Haan. It is a recognition that we are relational by divine design and function. In consequence, community and relationality have theological significance. Human relations are the reflection of a God-who-relates. To choose exemption from the community because of fearful defensiveness is to ignore not only the negotiable interests of others, but the moral "form of the personal," the way that we know the God-who-relates.

Gustafson moves away from Haan's psychological purchase on relationality, joining Macmurray's emphasis on the theological significance of relationships. In the belief in an immanent and communicative God, the human person sees the activity of God in relationships, as the Creator is in the interdependence of life. Gustafson points out that the analogy has its limits, however, in that no person ought ever to presume to know directly the indicative or the imperative of God's action. Those limits do not preclude a discernment that centers on God, but they do qualify Macmurray's analogy. One of the distinctive modifications which Gustafson provides for both Haan's and Macmurray's articulations of relationality is the maxim of moral discernment that one ought to "relate things in a manner appropriate to their relations to God."[35] For Haan, belief in this maxim would be a theoretical (and unscientific) leap; for Macmurray, less so. Haan is more concerned with the specific dynamics between persons, and though Macmurray can see the theological significance of relationality, neither would speculate on the relations of agents to God as a baseline for moral discernment.

Of the three interactionists, Gustafson has the most comprehensive considerations on community as a moral category. Haan's notion of community is undeveloped as a category in and of itself, despite her debt to Alexander Sesonske, and her dependence on group dynamics in testing. Community is more developed in Macmurray's thought than it is in Haan's, where it is simply a respect of others' rights and interests. For Macmurray, community is a response to a divine design by which persons "apprehending and enjoying a world outside of ourselves in company with others" see in their relations the reflection of a God-who-relates. Gustafson has relatively little to say about community outside of a theological context. He does note, however, in building his case for a theological community of moral discourse, that one need not rely upon theological categories to acknowledge the value of the communal form of moral discernment:

> To demythologize such an affirmation, we have simply the commonplace observation that discourse and deliberation between informed and serious men is more likely to lead to action that is fitting and ethically defensible than are other procedures.[36]

But the best representation of Gustafson's thought on community is a theological one. In remarkable coincidence with Macmurray, community for Gustafson is, first and foremost, a locus of God's activity, a place where interaction with others is given an added theological dimension:

> From the experience of others or of otherness, [community], for reasons of heart and mind, respects and reveres *an* Other; it acknowledges dependence upon and gratitude to *an* Other; it develops a sense of obligation to *an* Other, and a sense of repentance in the face of its failure to relate properly to *the* Other.[37]

Beyond Macmurray, Gustafson examines the actual functioning of the specific community. The community takes up the purposes of God—creating, sustaining, restraining, and making better the quality of life in three specific areas: the ethos of the culture in which it finds itself, the interpersonal relationships within it, and the institutions to which it relates.[38] Community takes up a collective charge to be the instrument of God. It has a mission of value to its members and their internal relations as well as to the "outside." In a manner consistent with his notion of discernment, Gustafson explains that the internal role of the community is less didactic than it is illuminative:

> The task of the church is not to tell them what [members] ought to do in specificity, but to enable them to see possibilities of moral value, and pitfalls of temptation in what they are doing and in what they can do.[39]

The outcome of this collective discernment is a formation of consensus in the community which, for all of its theological underpinnings, is not unlike Haan's notion of equalization. Taking into account the community's "readings" of the course for moral action, the community collaboratively perceives what God is enabling and requiring and determines an adequately balanced moral response.

Finally, in Gustafson's process of communal discernment, open participation is critical. With a combination of the insights of both Macmurray and Haan regarding participation—active agency and unimpeded contribution—Gustafson expounds participation especially in relation to the role of the minister in the community:

> The authority of the religious expert is not granted by virtue of his knowledge and ordination, and therefore neither quiet assent not vigorous obedience is forthcoming. The leader becomes a person whose function it is to give guidance to a consensus-forming pro-

cess, in and through which particular judgments (including his own) can be clarified and brought to bear on the relevant points of action.[40]

In promoting participation, and in a manner reminiscent of both Haan and Macmurray in which all actively contribute and none (including the minister) dominates, the community engages in a moral discourse that is truly collegial:

> Discourse involves mutual probing, each participant with his special skills, his gifts for wisdom, his technical knowledge, his powers of persuasion, enlightening the process toward consensus about what deeds and words are consonant with the faith, what performances are consistent with and expressive of the beliefs of the church.[41]

Reinforcing Haan's finding that led groups had more adequate moral action and growth than dominated groups, Gustafson's theory of participation prescribes a minister who has enough confidence in God's presence within the community that all participants in the moral discourse will have a voice.

An assertion that reflects a synthesis of the themes of relationality and community in Haan, Macmurray, and Gustafson will show how their perspectives affirm, complement, coincide with, and critique each other. But the theological significance of relationality and community held by Macmurray and Gustafson are distinctive positive contributions that are not treated by Haan. These theological modifications and amendments to her perspective are critical to our proposal of a theological project in service of the life of the church. In regard to relationality and community: *All human persons are social beings. No fitting moral action may be discerned in isolation from its effects on other agents. We propose, therefore, a relational ethic derived through communal participative dialogue wherein that which God enables and requires may come to be known.*

V. The Role of Belief in God and Jesus Christ

We have gleaned a central insight about morality from Haan and fortified it and critiqued it with other perspectives. In addition to methodological amendments, Macmurray and Gustafson have proved to be strong partners in the discussion intended to advance notions of Christian ethics and pastoral practice. By sharing Haan's interactional affirmations and articulating the role of religious belief in the moral life, they help demonstrate the applicability of Haan's insight to our project. In giving special attention to this Christian congruence with Haan's interactional perspective, we may further explicate a theological dimension in the work of James Gustafson, preserving the belief that God and Christ are at the center of the moral life.

Three central aspects of Gustafson's moral theology are important for the integration of the interactional proposal and Christian belief. First, we recall a linchpin of "theocentric ethics," that in moral considerations all things must be related in a manner appropriate to their relations to God. While hardly a material principle clarifying specific situations, this guideline nevertheless allows for a certain convergence of psychological and spiritual considerations in the discernment process. The maxim may put a burden on the agent who is not omniscient regarding all things' relations to God, but it evokes in the moral imagination of the believer a healthy humility about the ultimate adequacy of justice and equity as they are humanly conceived.

God becomes the locus of ethics, a prior reality who pervades any discernment of the good and right thing to do. Such theocentricity is a freeing as well as a binding truth. It reflects the radical freedom of a reformed or even existentialist Christian perspective, for we may discern and act with confidence that God's creative and redemptive love takes precedence over our human aspirations toward justice and justification. Yet, this truth is also binding, for moral discernment and action are not entirely comprehended by the description of psychological dynamics, which Gustafson might dismiss as "androcentric" in their orientation.

Second, religious belief affects the shape and content of one's morality in ways which the dynamics of interaction alone do not. Belief in God engenders "senses" of God that in turn give rise to moral discernment and action. For example, if one has a sense of the undeserved goodness of God to oneself, in gratitude, one passes that goodness along to others in similar fashion. As Gustafson illustrates,

> Gratitude as a reason of mind and heart for being moral has been a deep and persistent one in the biblical communities and in the life and thought of the church. "Freely you have received, freely give" is more than a convenient saying to induce churchgoers to place money in an offering basket during worship. The comma,

in a sense, covers the fulcrum of a way of life. In its affective dimensions, the sense of gratitude moves the will to act.[42]

The same may be said of other "senses" of God. Because of these senses of God, the believing agent may be transformed in disposition and character to become a person of gratitude, repentance, and possibility, for example.

Belief can also influence moral discernment and action through the believing community's interpretation of specific events using traditional religious symbols and language. A symbol such as the cross or language such as the "paschal mystery" offers the believer other considerations in moral determinations. The symbol or language may reveal features of the issue yet undisclosed, or offer distinctive substance to the discernment of Christian agents, a substance not subsumed in the psychological or philosophical interactional proposals.

Third, belief in Jesus Christ, essential to Christianity, affects the moral life. Gustafson provides little explanation for what really constitutes "belief."[43] Of particular interest and difficulty is the relative inconsistency between the centrality of Christ in *Christ and the Moral Life* and the minimal role that Christ has in the moral life articulated in *Ethics from a Theocentric Perspective*. Gustafson states that belief in Christ entails for the agent a difference in perspective and posture. The intentions or future orientations of the believer are affected by belief in Christ, as the disciple tests the consistency of intended action against his or her faith in the Jesus of tradition and scripture.

Finally, belief in Christ provides a difference in the understanding of moral norms in the believer through the creative application of the message of Christ's teaching found in the love command or the parables, for example. Christ illuminates a moral path in teachings and norms and enables the journey on that path by the formation and transformation of the perspectives, postures, dispositions, and intentions of the believing agent. Christ provides actual content to the moral interaction of believers, and, as a powerful locus of personal strength and transformation, Christ is a resource for moral action.

The Christological element in the construction of a foundational ethic for pastoral moral discernment is critical, as it modifies the contours of the interactional proposal so that it may be employed in the Christian setting. *For the Christian, the moral response is centered on God's relationship to the human person and the person's relationship to God. The actual content of the believer's morality—dispositions, interpretations of experience, and normative considerations—are shaped by belief in Jesus Christ. Christian believers look to Christ as the one who illuminates and empowers a moral response to God's relationship with us.*

*   *   *

We have completed the first of our two-part task of constructing a foundational ethic and developing a critical method for pastoral moral discernment. In the conversation among the three interactional perspectives, we have clarified the contributions of each to a comprehensive foundational ethic. Although Haan's insight about the interactional nature of morality remains as the base for our constructed ethic, Macmurray and Gustafson contribute to the five assertions describing the features of our ethic. That foundational ethic as we have established it is *historical* in its method; *multidimensional* in its moral anthropology; *imaginative* and *creative* in its resolutions toward a course for action; *social, relational,* and *communal* in its perspectival approach; and *centered on our relationship to God in Christ.*

NOTES

1. Haan, "An Interactional Morality of Everyday Life," in *Social Science As Moral Inquiry*, 230–231.
2. Macmurray, *Persons in Relation*, 22.
3. Macmurray, *The Self As Agent*, 217.
4. Gustafson, *Can Ethics Be Christian?*, 12.
5. Gustafson, *Ethics from a Theocentric Perspective*, 135–136.
6. Gustafson, *Theology and Christian Ethics*, 42.
7. Haan, et al., *On Moral Grounds: The Search for Practical Morality*, 348.
8. Ibid., 349.
9. Ibid., 349–350.
10. Haan and her associates set out to test the cognitive proposal of Kohlberg, who asserted an irreversible invariant sequence of stages of moral development, each of which constituted a certain kind of "character." Haan's findings are offered in relation to the adequacy of Kohlberg's stage-as-character concept. We will return to a theological discussion of character in Chapter 6.
11. See Haan, *On Moral Grounds*, 150–151.
12. Ibid., 151.
13. Ibid., 214.
14. Macmurray, *Freedom in the Modern World*, 170–175.
15. Ibid., 55.
16. Macmurray, *The Self As Agent*, 196.

17.   Macmurray makes a distinction between motivation, a long-term moral disposition grounded in the "love and fear" scheme above, and intention, which is the moral impetus for a particular action.

18.   See the discussion in *The Self As Agent*, 194–196.

19.   Ibid., 197–198.

20.   Gustafson, *Ethics from a Theocentric Perspective*, Volume 1, 274.

21.   Ibid., 118–119.

22.   Gustafson, *Can Ethics Be Christian?*, 47.

23.   Ibid., 29.

24.   Haan, et al., *On Moral Grounds*, 67.

25.   Ibid.

26.   Gustafson, *Theology and Christian Ethics*, 100–101.

27.   Ibid., 39ff.

28.   Ibid.

29.   Haan, "Moral Development and Action From a Social Constructivist Perspective," 3.

30.   Haan, "Moral Development and Action," 22.

31.   Haan does acknowledge an indebtedness to Alexander Sesonske, who sees community as the starting point for morality, but she does not develop the idea. See Alexander Sesonske, *Value and Obligation: The Foundation of an Empiricist Ethical Theory* (Berkeley: University of California Press, 1957).

32.   See Chapters 7 and 15, respectively, of Haan, et al., *On Moral Grounds*.

33.   Macmurray, *Persons in Relation*, 51.

34.   Macmurray, *Freedom in the Modern World*, 170–175.

35.   Gustafson, *Ethics from a Theocentric Perspective*, Vol. 2, 298.

36.   Gustafson, *The Church as Moral Decision-Maker*, 85.

37.   Gustafson, *Ethics from a Theocentric Perspective*, Volume One, 135–136.

38.   Gustafson, *The Church as Moral Decision-Maker*, 66–70.

39.   Ibid., 35–36.

40.   Ibid., 130–131.

41.   Ibid., 154.

42.   Gustafson, *Can Ethics Be Christian?*, 101.

43.   Indeed, he may be referring to "piety" under which faith is subsumed. See the discussion in *Ethics from a Theocentric Perspective*, Vol. 1, 201–204.

6

PRACTICAL IMPLICATIONS:
Toward a Critical Method of Catholic
Pastoral Moral Discernment

We began this project by delineating a problem for Catholic pastoral practice and moral theology. The absence or at least inadequacy of theories and methods of moral discernment in Catholic pastoral settings is an especially pertinent issue for the post-Conciliar Church, which has sought to renew its approach to pastoral care and moral theology. With a view to strengthening Catholic moral theology by effectively incorporating an underutilized source, psychology, and by including complementary sources, we have proposed elements of a comprehensive foundational ethic that may serve as a basis for pastoral moral discernment: the consideration of a personal situation in a Catholic ministerial setting by which a course of moral action is determined. We turn our final attention to a method for this discernment. Relying on the five theoretical assertions that we forged from the interactional sources, we will now draw forth their practical implications to suggest how discernment may proceed in pastoral situations.

One conceptual framework for pastoral moral discernment has been articulated in various official Church documents. If we were to characterize the underlying ethical method of that framework, we would say that it is principally deontological in its approach. The pastoral interpretation or translation of a document is largely a matter of determining the believer's ability to measure up to the stipulations of a moral command or duty as they are promulgated by a uniquely competent magisterium. "Pastoral" becomes a code word for certain allowances and leniencies in determining culpability but has little to do with respect for the integrity of the individual who does not immediately recognize and embrace the moral commands that are promulgated by the magisterium. To demonstrate the relative adequacy of such pastoral moral discernment and its underlying ethical method, we will finally outline and critique it as it appears in a document of central importance in the life of the post-Conciliar Church, Paul VI's encyclical on the regulation of human birth, *Humanae Vitae*.

As with any proposal of a practical method in ministry, we do not purport to address every aspect of sound moral discernment, nor are we interested in the development of a step-by-step system for the activity of discernment. We cannot hope to develop a method so complete that it replaces the revered art of moral reflection in pastoral care. The critical method of pastoral moral discernment proposed here, even in its nascent form, elucidates elements to which one must attend in sound moral discernment and is a contribution to Catholic moral theory and practice.

I. A Historical Worldview: Discernment and Experience

The acceptance of a historical worldview transforms the very nature of moral discernment, as well as the expectations that moral agents have for discernment. With a closed, monolithic, static, objective world order as the point of departure, moral discernment is in reality the mere application of principles to the endless variety of events and exigencies in life. The interpretation that is required in such applications can be fairly reduced to a deductive activity whereby the particular circumstances of a given life constitute the minor premise of a logical syllogism, which serves as the conceptual framework for the settling of cases of conscience. There are, of course, contingencies and situations from real life that do not immediately lend themselves to classification according to the first principles of a syllogism. There are remainders when the division into moral categories is completed.

With the affirmation of a historical worldview, moral discernment becomes a different undertaking. If we admit that change, development, evolution, formation, and transformation, for example, are the essential elements of life; and that time is not the medium through which an objective moral order plays itself out but the chronicle of God's salvation of humanity, then discernment becomes a genuine interpretation of God's ways and our response to those ways. That interpretation has its attendant difficulties. It is not nearly so clean and orderly as the syllogistic determinations of moral wrongfulness that serve the classicist worldview. It requires attention to the experience and development of the individual moral agent, to the agent's particular circumstances, to the timing of the moral decision, and the determination and execution of appropriate action as the continuance of history. As none of these elements may be immediately clear, a real discernment with all its possible pitfalls must ensue. To take history seriously is to make awesome demands on moral discernment.

Pastoral moral discernment must directly account for the *experience* of the believer. If one assents to the basic idea that the events of history constitute God's involvement in the lives of believers, then an individual's account of his or her experience in life carries a freight of significance that requires recall and attention in times of discernment. This account is more than a mere chronology. It is a story of events, situations, relationships, turning points, setbacks, achievements, former discernments, and decisions—all of which require selection and interpretation. If we take history seriously, it is ultimately a story of faith, a new purchase on God's involvement in the human arena. Heuristic devices and images may be applied to the individual, discrete events and to the account as a whole. The effects of relating and interpreting the experience of the believer are manifold, but certainly one major outcome is the establishment or reinforcement of the idea that a person's life is a unique unfolding of God's good and creative intentions, and that the believer may rely on the evidence of such past involvement to look to help discern the situation at hand.

Practically speaking, the role of the pastoral minister in engendering a sense of "holy history" as a resource for moral discernment is to elicit the account of one's experience and to assist in its interpretation. An educed autobiography qualified by the perspective of faith can serve as a critical starting point for moral discernment because it points to the enduring truth that God's locus of activity is not restricted to the overtly religious moments of life such as worship, appropriation of doctrine, or rare instances of meditation. The presence and action of God can be appreciated in all the events of life and, more generally, in all of human history.

An appreciation of personal experience has particular force in determining the role that norms and principles play in pastoral moral discernment.[1] As synthetic statements of the collective wisdom of believers, norms and principles serve as one expression of the experience of God in history. Because they represent traditional moral experience in condensed form, they help to consolidate the discernment process by offering to the discerner general guidance to save him or her from treating each situation as wholly new. The pastoral minister does well to incorporate them into discernment, and there are times when such incorporation is especially incumbent on the minister as the representative of a community steeped in a particular identity.

Indeed, interactional pastoral discernment is best described as a co-construction of a course of moral action. With this in mind, in upholding the traditions of the Christian community, the minister cannot afford to hold a value-neutral stance in hopes that the agent will simply arrive at a moral determination, or a bluntly instructional stance, from which the agent will appropriate correct values. There are, of course, risks involved in co-constructive discernment. Dysfunctional relations among the participants or poor prior formation of the participants in a corrupt or inadequate moral environment can subvert the process. An honest standoff can occur. Thus the art of pastoral assistance with discernment lies in the minister accurately representing the values and claims of the community, but with a sensitivity and a respect for the views of the agent.

Norms and principles ought not bear more weight than is their due in pastoral moral discernment.[2] In light of the primacy granted to the historical worldview over a classicist worldview, a model of pastoral moral discernment that commences from norms and principles will in most situations prove wanting. To the extent that norms and principles can be assimilated into moral discernment as expressions of experience they will assist the discernment. Insofar as the minister insists that they are the touchstone of the discernment process because they somehow serve as the connection to an objective moral order that exists outside history, they may very well hamstring the discernment.

With a historically grounded ethic at its base, pastoral moral discernment must also attend to the *moral development* of the discerning agent. This may emerge in the form of a discerner's autobiography. What is at stake is the agent's capacity for the appreciation of certain positions and for carrying out particular courses of moral action. Judgment on the part of the minister as to the agent's capacities, even with the active involvement of the discerner, is not an easy task. There is no shortage of theories to which one may subscribe in determining the moral maturity of an individual. Although we have sought to demonstrate the relative advantage of the social interactional proposal, our purpose here is not to suggest its use as a diagnostic device. (Indeed, Haan would shun the use of it for such purposes. Much of the impetus for her revision of Kohlberg's scheme was the desire to introduce a more fluid, less tightly structured system to describe moral development and action. Diagnosis becomes more tentative by design in the interactional proposal.)

In accepting a changing, evolving world in which God is present in the events of life, we can move confidently in accepting the moral development of the agent as a critical consideration. The minister needs to gauge in some way the present moral maturity of the agent, and insofar as is possible, the history and the future of that growth, in order to provide a context for the particular discernment at hand. Former attempts to describe "pastoral" moral discernment included categories such as "invincible ignorance" in an effort to appropriate the issue of the moral capacity of the agent. Such a minimalist approach does not suffice. A more adequate model of discernment, one that is not strictly interested in loopholes in principles nor in the relative culpability of the agent, must account in a positive and nuanced fashion for the unique history of the individual.[3]

As one begins to incorporate a theory of moral development into the discernment method, another dimension of a critical model of pastoral moral discernment emerges. With due respect to the history and moral development of the agent, pastoral moral discernment is integrated into the life of the believer as an ongoing process. As such, pastoral moral discernment may be more akin to spiritual direction than to casuistry, attending to the larger picture of one's life with special heed paid to its moral dimensions over time. By encouraging and participating in a model of discernment in which the historical continuity of the agent is important, the pastoral minister can be of more assistance on occasions of moral dilemma and crisis. Relying on knowledge of the ongoing response of the agent to God's initiative, the minister is not reduced to legal advice-giver, to counselor for crisis intervention, or to sacramental functionary. Ideally, pastoral moral discernment informed by history becomes less an intervention and more an accompaniment in the life of the believer.

All three of the interactional theorists to which we have appealed as sources for our foundational ethic support the notion that moral impulses must be translated into action in order to qualify as truly moral. From Haan's stress on the everyday quality of our dialogical interactions, from Macmurray's turn to the "I do" position, and from Gustafson's insistence that agency is constituted in one's ability to follow through on intentions, we have concluded that action, the discrete unit of history, is the validating facet of morality. Effective strategies for practical action must be a part of the determinations of pastoral moral discernment. That is, the discernment must *culminate in action*.

This implication is perhaps painfully obvious to any pastoral minister who has had to wrestle with the often central question of one seeking assistance with moral discernment: "What should I do?" Nevertheless, pointed designation of the necessity for culmination in action as an important feature of our model of discernment seems warranted because by locating a criterion for adequate moral discernment in practical action, we avoid the deficiency of the strictly analytical schemes of philosopher-kings, unassailable logic that is only remotely connected to the situation at hand. By holding ourselves to this standard of praxis, moral theology enjoys the prospect of being transformed from an antiseptic enterprise of juggling principles to a theological reflection on the actual moral balances which believers must strike in discernment directed toward action.

II. A Multivalent Moral Anthropology: Interdependence, Intuition, Analysis, and Character

Each of the three interactional moralists affirms a view of humanity in which the person is an agent who can fashion responses to the events of life. The agent is one who makes specific responses drawing on the resources of emotion and intuition as well as intellect and who forms enduring qualities, traits, or skills that can be practiced, honed, and transferred to new situations demanding moral responses. This moral anthropology suggests certain guiding principles for methods of pastoral moral discernment. Moreover, the procedures for discernment that it implies may be contrasted to the latent and manifest moral anthropology and model for discernment that one encounters in various Church documents, including *Humanae Vitae*.

In affirming a positive moral anthropology as a hallmark of our foundational ethic, we prescribe a certain *perspectival trust* on the part of both minister and discerner in pastoral moral discernment.[4] This prescription may sound disingenuous to those who assume such trust will automatically exist in a sensitive relationship such as pastoral moral discernment, yet it bears explicit pronouncement in the face of contrasting moral anthropologies, which emphasize a fundamental selfishness, ignorance, or value neutrality in the human condition. These anthropologies make ample room for deontological or didactic modes of pastoral moral discernment because the minister has little or no assurance that the agent, left to his or her own resources, will ever arrive at a sound course of moral action. To see the human person in the positive light of the interactional perspective is to propose an environment of trust in discernment in which both minister and discerner can afford to initiate and receive, talk and listen.

The human person must be regarded in moral matters as one who responds on emotional, intuitional, and intellectual levels. Pastoral moral discernment must *account for factors that are not strictly rational*. For example, the attention to emotions in decision making and moral action is an apt means of approach to the complex issue of moral motivation. Haan has noted the enabling and disabling effects of "coping" and "defending" techniques in moral dialogues fueled by emotional states. Similarly, Macmurray theorizes about emotional reason, whereby one makes unabashedly evaluative statements based on judgments denounced in critical philosophy as undependable emotional preferences. Gustafson looks to moral senses such as gratitude and direction, described as combinations of emotions and perceptions, to inform and even motivate moral discernment. The conscientious pastoral minister does well to attend to these potential lubricants or frictions for moral discernment, not because such attention makes for a better environment of empathic regard but because a higher quality of moral decision making is the result.

When one admits emotion as a potent factor in determining moral action, pastoral moral discernment may be conducted with special deference to the emotions and intuitions as apprehensions that are possible without apparent reflective rationality.[5] Practically speaking, the minister must employ methods that evoke these emotional-moral connections in the believer without manipulating them. One recommendation, which comes as no surprise to a seasoned pastoral minister, is that discussions of virtue, morality, transformation, conversion, and discipleship can be generated readily on the emotional level of sensibilities and intuitions through the effective incorporation of stories, parables, and scriptural and non-scriptural narratives. Such storytelling is often the technique of the best pastoral ministers who, in efforts to support and challenge the faithful, rely more on their ability to provide an interpretive context for a particular issue than on their ability to make a persuasive presentation of propositional material about a given issue. We say this technique is "speaking to the heart," and the subsequent change, enlightenment, and discernment are based on the hearer's "reasons of the heart," which are much more emotive and intuitive than intellectual, analytical, and deductive.

We do not gainsay the role of the intellectual, rational, and analytical capacities in moral decision making. Though all interactional theorists see the strictly rational as only one facet of a comprehensive moral determination, none negates the importance of those elements in moral discernment. However, their conception of the mode of access to the rational factors of moral decision making is distinctive in that one comes to moral decisions through dialogue with another and not in the privacy of one's mind. Each theorist still maintains a view of the human person that esteems the elements of cognition associated with rationality. These elements of a method of discernment imply, for example, *a respect for facts, the sound construction of an argument and an appreciation for its logical validity, and the careful use of language that both describes and prescribes.*

One of the clear points of separation and distinction among the interactionists with regard to moral anthropology is the role of character. In choosing a course that admittedly weaves among the theorists, we have synthesized this element of our foundational ethic as a "relatively stable individual history," which engenders responses that may be "characteristic," but are "open to change, renewal, and transformation." While not adhering to traditional terms such as virtues or habits, we do grant that there are some enduring features of a person's moral constitution, some elements of a personal history, which carry over from one situation to the next. These do not predict the moral performance of a person but describe, in Gustafson's words, "conditions which make possible and likely certain sorts of actions."[6] The overriding practical importance of the existence of character, though, does not lie in the minister's resulting ability to foresee or ensure a given course of action for the agent. In the consideration of a discerner's character or moral history, the discerner and the minister *attend to the person as a moral agent.* If the task of a therapeutic setting involves recounting and reconstituting the person as a psyche or personality that has emerged from particular genetic and environmental influences and which continues to evolve, the task of pastoral moral discernment involves recounting and reconstituting the person as a constellation of moral qualities that has emerged in the course of experience, decisions, and other uncontrollable factors, and which continues to evolve.

The practical import of character for our proposed method is found in this turn toward the agent. Particularly if an occasion of pastoral moral discernment is prompted by the settling of a question, dilemma, or case, but even if the discernment is an ongoing one, a requisite base for reflection includes at least some moral portrait of the discerning person and, ideally, a portrait of others who are involved in the process or outcome of the discernment. This depiction of the person-as-moral-agent may come to light, both for the discerner and the minister, in the course of dialogue. But a request on the part of the minister for the discerner to "characterize" himself or herself as a moral agent would be a directly helpful technique, both for the minister and the agent. With due respect, the minister may inquire about personal history or development with a view toward the articulation of a moral picture of the person. This self-generated description is susceptible to prevarications, which are not of paramount concern. The particular attempt to move the discernment away from the issue at hand to probing self-description is guided by the effort to frame the discernment as a moment in the development of a person, a step in the successful resolution of an issue.[7]

III. Subjectivity, Creativity, and Induction: The Role of the Individual in Discernment

Although room has been made in Catholic casuistry for conscience and the internal forum, few explanations regarding subjective considerations have been offered. In much Catholic teaching, and even in the suggested pastoral translation of that teaching, there seems to be a subtle but pervasive distrust of the individual, the particular, the inductive, and the imaginative, accompanied by a corresponding credence in the collective, the universal, the deductive, and the procedural.

Haan's theory is perhaps strongest in its affirmation of the particular dynamics of a situation; for her, the solution of a given moral contretemps is bounded by few if any considerations of universal principles or even by the relatively fixed moral convictions of the agent or agents involved. Macmurray views the individual subject as capable of authoring satisfactory moral determinations based on the personal resource of emotional reason. Gustafson's accent, after reading the moral situation by means of imagination, interpretation, possibilities, sensitivities, and empathy, suggests an acceptance and even preponderance of the subjective, creative, and inductive capacities of the agent in sound moral discernment.

With special regard for the practical nature of discernment, this feature of our ethic suggests that creativity, the special capacity of humans to interpret, design, plan, formulate, and produce, will play a critical role in that discernment. Without resorting to an overly instrumental understanding of the adequacy of moral determinations, we may recall Haan's disarming criterion for adequacy: Does it work? Her criterion implies that *moral determinations in a pastoral setting should be appropriate to the host of claims to which discerners find themselves subject, and that the act of articulating, setting priorities, adjudicating, and acting on those claims will require not merely an analytical but a synthetic, multifaceted, and yet singular response, commonly termed "creative."*

Like music, sculpture, or drama, the moral determination is the fruit of a subjective appropriation, interpretation, and representation of diverse facets of the demands of a situation. Moral discernment is more an art than a science, and as such, it draws upon the aesthetic and sensual, for instance. It is like a great work of art. Just as Bach is not Schoenberg and Pollock is not Degas, so the moral determination has a quality that is uniquely responsive to the interior movements of an agent. Moral discernment is an act of giving birth to the unique expression of ideas, feelings, and perceptions. The role of the pastoral minister in this creative process, then, is more maieutic than didactic, is better depicted as a midwife than pedagogue.

Material for such a creative process is that from which art is conceived—images. The imagination forms visions of truth which in turn shape a particular, concrete expression of the way life is. According to our interactional theorists, who see the importance of subjectivity, we can say of moral discernment as we say of art, that imagination is essential. Imagination is a potent force for recapitulating the past, interpreting the present, and envisioning the future.[8] The images may be in the form of symbols, stories, or scenarios. They may involve the discerner on the emotional, intellectual, or aesthetic levels. The images may be the fruit of momentary insights or extended musings. They may be projected into the past or the future, and concern themselves with causes or consequences. Given the essential role of the imagination, the task of the discerner and the pastoral minister is to *generate, elicit, present, and critique images* that serve to inform and transform the discernment and, ultimately, the discerner.[9]

Of interest to this discussion of the role of subjectivity and its various forms in moral discernment is Haan's contention that a key factor in conducting a dialogue toward equalization is that parties in the balancing process make known to each other their own *self-interests*. Anticipating the fallout from such a bold statement, which upon first hearing seems to run against the grain of most moral theories, Haan notes the contribution which moral psychology might make in this regard:

> Since theorists have assumed that morality is achieved when self-interest is replaced by interest in others and interest in society, self-interest has not had legitimacy. Since psychologists customarily focus on individual welfare (often to the exclusion of general welfare), their move to investigate morality may cast a different light on the role of self-interest in morality. . . . The dialogue winnows self-interest to decide on the legitimacy or illegitimacy of each participant's claims.[10]

The moral philosopher's or theologian's appropriately skeptical question in response would be, "How can people know what their true self-interests are?" (Haan all but dismisses the query with the answer, "Whatever they perceive them to be."[11]) There seems to be merit to the idea that expressed self-interest, in both its legitimate and even deluded forms, must be an integral part of the discernment process. A moral determination that denies personal autonomy to the discerner or other parties is no moral determination at all. Much violence can be done in the name of dissolving valid self-interests into a universalized notion of the good or the right. Indeed, the whole thrust of accounting for subjective factors in moral discernment is that extant moral systems often fall short in addressing individual persons and situations. While we nod in agreement that an agent's subjective creativity and imagination can contribute to sound moral discernment, we usually stop short of affirming self-interests as important subjective ingredients in the moral determination. Because we are afraid that autonomy too easily degenerates into selfishness, individual talents, gifts, and perspectives are often sacrificed to a generalized but unexamined notion of the universalized good.[12] The practical implication of the importance of self-interest for a method of pastoral moral discernment is relatively straightforward. The tone of the encounter between minister and discerner should be one that encourages the discerner to express self-interests, well grounded or shallow though they may be. The effectiveness of the process and outcome of the moral dialogue depends on all parties making known their own perspectives, claims, perceived rights, and notions of justice. Inopportune moralizing on the part of the minister could abort the expression of such self-interests, and a subterfuge of real discernment could result.

For a provisional summary of this section on the implications of the subjective, creative, and inductive elements of our foundational ethic, we look again to Gustafson's category of "the fitting," which he borrowed from H. Richard Niebuhr.[13] A determined moral action that accounts for personal imagination, possibilities, interpretation, sensibilities, and faith, the "fitting" is a direct answer to Gustafson's guiding question in the moral life, "What is God enabling and requiring in this situation?" It exacts from both the discerner and the minister in pastoral moral discernment *a careful attention to the subjective interpretations of a situation so that a response or a solution may emerge from the process that respects the unique situation and claims of the moral agent.*

IV. A Relational Ethic, A Moral Community: The Role of Social Interaction in Discernment

At the outset of our project, we established warrants for the use of experience, empirical science, and psychology to ground Catholic moral theology and paved the way for appropriating the insights of the social interactional proposal for pastoral moral discernment. We have confined our thesis to modest claims about the pastoral discernment process in the Catholic tradition, stopping short of drawing out the implications of relationality for theory and method in the larger enterprise of moral theology itself. We can see in the tenets of interactional theory, whether psychological, philosophical, or theological, the prospects for continuing the exciting post-Conciliar renewal of moral theology. Simply put, if we attend more to the ways in which the moral life is played out every day in the "basic unit" of morality— the relationship—we can more effectively cultivate a discipline to which believers can lend credence and from which they can receive help in living out the demands of Christian faith. While it is not our purpose to come full circle with the implications of relationality as a foundation for Catholic moral theology, we can point out that such a move from empirical insight to a "morally charged" pastoral practice could provide a new horizon for moral theology. Following the cues of a theology which is grounded in interpreted relational experience, we can see the suggestion of a new method in moral theology, one which seeks the data of pastoral experience prior to the formulation of moral teaching.[14]

In affirming the dialectical nature of the moral life, moral discernment and decision making are promoted as *a dialogue that occurs in the creative tension between a moral problem, dilemma, or decision and its resolution.* Just as scholars cannot fully know the shape or outcome of their thoughts until they are committed to an audience of conversation which responds to the thoughts with affirmation, nuance, and amendment, the discerner looks to dialogue as the form which is also the content of the moral life. In dialogue the discerner makes real the impulse to reach some "equalization," as Haan would have it. In conversation with the pastoral minister, the discerner represents all of the applicable dimensions of a given "position" and with good faith enters into a dialectic in which the position is affirmed, refined, amended, or challenged by the minister. The premise of interactional morality is that through such an exchange and its ensuing interpretations and reformulations, a sound discernment may be made. Such discernment requires of the minister a conviction that a quality resolution may be achieved in the exchange. The basic practical implication of this relational conception is that with due respect for both the subjective soundings of the individual and the incumbent representative role of the minister, the basic methodological shape of pastoral moral discernment is an intentional dialogue aimed at achieving a moral balance by which the discerner and the minister can abide and live.

The value of dialogue as the mode of discernment is especially evident in considering the possibility of self-deception. By offering to the minister a subjective assessment of a situation, the discerner is able to test its adequacy. Because of such a test of adequacy, Macmurray has great confidence in his notion of "emotional reason." He can posit the importance of individual value judgments not because they are a flawless source of moral discernment, but because he has already set a relational foundation to stand as a corrective to faulty judgment. With the ascendancy of the "I and You" position and the concomitant skepticism about the "I think" position, the clear suggestion is that between the "I" and the "You" will be an important "winnowing," as Haan calls it, by which self-deception is challenged and corrected.

Under the rubric of interactional morality, the most appropriate term for the exchange is *participation*. For Haan, all members of the dialogue contribute in unimpeded fashion. There is free and honest interaction, and none enjoys a veto power over possible outcomes of the dialogue. For Macmurray, participation refers to the mode in which a moral agent is in the world—not as object and observer but as subject and participant. So, drawing on Haan's and Macmurray's appropriation of the concept of participation, we allow that certain qualities to the dialogue will influence the practical shape of pastoral moral discernment, namely active agency and unimpeded contribution. The discerner, who must take responsibility for the outcome of the discernment, is not the student or directee of the minister but an agent, an actor, a mover. Consistent with this belief, the positions of the discerner must be articulated freely and received by the minister throughout the dialogue, without judgments that promote "defending" mechanisms and inhibit "coping" mechanisms.

For Gustafson, the role of the minister in a discernment process must be to provide guidance toward a formation of consensus, which stands as both the product and the evidence of a clarification process. Moreover, the minister is not an expert by virtue of position or ordination, but one whose interest in the welfare of the discerner makes his or her participation particularly apt and valuable.[15] However, the minister's role in pastoral moral discernment is not reduced to a facilitator or animator. In light of the particular *communal context* that prevails, the minister represents truth claims that cannot be diluted in deference to the non-judgmentalism which is helpful to the expression of positions in the dialogue. Our three theorists vary in their understanding of the impact of community upon the moral life. We turn to Gustafson for the explication of the communal aspect of our foundational ethic because his is the most detailed description of community, the most theological in its concern, and the most directly applicable to the project in this chapter.

Because the community is the present locus of God's creating, sustaining, restraining, and promoting life, the community receives its charge to tend to the ethos of culture, to the institutions to which it relates, and to the quality of the interpersonal relationships within it. In doing so, the community itself develops certain truth claims which are the fruit of the formation of a moral consensus. *The role of the minister is to illuminate the truth claims of the community.* The practical implications of this tenet cut two ways. To "illuminate" is not to assume an authoritarian or intractable position. On the other hand, the minister fails in his or her role if truth claims are not sufficiently illuminated, or if they are abandoned by the minister in the face of opposition simply because they may be difficult to realize. The community is ultimately identified by its intentional value, and *the minister fails the community if the memory, the wisdom, the teaching, the symbols, and the narrative that shape the intentional values are not represented to its members, especially at times of moral crossroads, confusion, and crisis.* Consequently, all participants, including the minister, are respected for their unique skills and perspectives in forging a consensus in discernment. But the minister, representing the intentional mission of the community, has the added responsibility of illuminating the truths that assemble the community in the first place, the realization of God's creating, sustaining, restraining, and promoting purposes for life. The ideal encounter is a productive dialogue in the context of the claims of the tradition and encouragement by the minister to live those claims.

V. A God-Centered Ethic: Discernment and Christian Belief

What about "that which assembles the community in the first place?" Amidst all of the above practical implications for pastoral moral discernment, what about the role of faith itself in the process of pastoral moral discernment? What are the practical implications of the aspects of faith to which we appealed in forming our foundational ethic: senses of God, a religious context for decision making, religious symbols, and language, the believer's relationship to Christ, and the use of scripture and tradition?

The discussion of the discerner's senses of God would serve several purposes in pastoral moral discernment. First, the invitation on the part of the minister to the discerner to review his or her "senses" of God is an invitation to confer in a manner more personal than the methods of speculative theology. A "sense" in Gustafson's terms is an affective and subjective experience of a God who lives in the life of the believer. Beginning discernment with such an invitation sends the clear signal that a personalized faith in God is the ground upon which any discernment rests. Important both for the discerner and for the minister is the discerner's articulation of the specific senses of God that are most eminent. All these senses may apply in a strictly theological grasp of the situation. But *in accounting for the sense or senses of God that are most predominant in the life of the discerner, the minister and the discerner may come to see the moral disposition which faith in God has engendered or could engender in the discerner.* The pervasive sense of God as giver of all good gifts has a different effect on the life of the believer, both historically and in the future, than an overwhelming sense of God as judge. Not only does such accounting locate the discernment firmly in the realm of faith; it also assists the minister in determining the spiritual bearings of the discerner.

Recapitulating in another way the importance of the senses of God, we conclude that *by grounding the discernment process in personalized faith in God, the minister is able to introduce a critical criterion of adequacy for discerning the good and right thing to do, specifically as that criterion is informed by faith: "All things must be related in a manner appropriate to their relations to God."* While this approach does not enjoy the quality of practical resolution often achieved in a teleological or deontological approach, it does keep before the discernment process an *ultimate frame of reference* which is critical and unique to a specifically pastoral setting.

Indeed, one of the current laments of ethicists is that institutions with limited horizons of value purport to develop their own ethical standards. For example, the corporate culture develops "business ethics," health care professions develop "biomedical ethics," the communications media develop "media ethics," and Congress, in dealing with its own, reduces the salient ethical issues to sexual conduct, public speaking fees, and bounced checks. With no ultimate or even adequate frame of reference for interpretation, "moral" action becomes procedural prudence within the given parameters of an institution.

Relating to things as they relate to God has an attendant difficulty, namely the lack of human omniscience. Nonetheless such relating lends to the *pastoral* discernment process a proper context for consideration. The less than ultimate values of family, friendship, professional advancement, or personal freedom, for example, find their true ability to disclose moral determinations when they are posed in relation to God. Without leveling or minimizing other factors in a sound moral discernment, the minister does well to propose such a standard of faith, perhaps in the form of Gustafson's signature question, "What is God enabling and requiring you to do?"

With the introduction of the senses of God and an ultimate frame of reference for interpreting a situation, we begin to see the role of faith in the moral discernment process. Recall, too, that in formulating our foundational ethic for discernment, we noted that *certain normative factors, which are ordinarily disclosed by religious symbols and religious language would also come into play for the discerning believer.* If such understandings are not articulated by the discerner, the minister should listen to and probe the discerner's relation to or imagination of specific Christian realities such as the incarnation, cross, resurrection, kingdom of God, as well as images from parables such as the prodigal son or the good Samaritan neighbor. Religious language, for example, of "witness," "discipleship," "grace," or "the redemption of the world" may also disclose to the discerner and the minister a light on the issue that only religious faith can provide.

We have characterized the "God-centeredness" of the foundational ethic for discernment as a *relationship between the believer and God through Jesus Christ by the power of the Spirit.* We note again the ways that Christ influences the moral discernment process. Belief in Christ results in a difference in the believer's disposition, that is, what Gustafson calls the perspective and posture of the believer; belief in Christ affects the intentions of the believer, both for this discernment and for the longer term; and Christ himself provides moral norms communicated through the message of his life. We have said further that the effect of these influences is that Christ serves as a source for moral formation and transformation of the discerner because of the transforming presence and power of the Holy Spirit. *Jesus Christ thus illuminates and empowers a response of the believer to God's grace and call.*[16]

The believer should test the consistency of an intended course of action against his or her own faith in the "Jesus of tradition and scripture." Although this testing is a central element in the development of a critical method of pastoral moral discernment, an extensive explication of it is beyond the scope of our concern here. The "Jesus of tradition" may include such diverse elements as the collective wisdom of the community of believers, the officially articulated truths of the magisterium, and insights wrought from theological reflection. Broaching the topic of the believer's notion of the "Jesus of scripture" and its impact on the discerner yields a focal point for the discernment process but also requires both creativity and methodological rigor. The minister who wants to raise the level of discourse beyond the discerner's possibly impressionistic reading of scripture may do well to be versed in thematic and categorical considerations of the relationship between scripture and the Christian moral life.[17] We infer from our foundational ethic that the minister involved in sound moral discernment in a Catholic pastoral setting must probe and incorporate the discerner's relationship to Jesus Christ, encountered in the normative sources of tradition and scripture and in the ongoing saving action of God in the everyday events of life.

VI. A Study in Contrast: The "Pastoral Directives" of Humanae Vitae and Interactional Pastoral Moral Discernment

On July 25, 1968, Pope Paul VI issued the encyclical *Humanae Vitae* on the regulation of birth in which he prohibited the use of artificial means of birth control by Roman Catholics. Its issuance prompted an unprecedented response of dissent from nearly every constituency of the Church, but perhaps most vocal among theologians and married laity. More than twenty years of theological reflection on the document itself and on the events surrounding its promulgation have yielded key insights about its widespread nonacceptance. An exhaustive review of that theological reflection is not our purpose here, but we do well to review two of those key insights as backdrops to our consideration of a specific part of *Humanae Vitae*, Section III, "Pastoral Directives."

Responses to *Humanae Vitae* may be roughly grouped according to two concerns, the "internal" adequacy of the argument regarding procreative ethics and the "external" argument based on the authority of the papal magisterium in demanding assent to the document. Many of the objections to the argument itself turned on the magisterium's natural law methodology in constructing a case against the use of artificial means of birth control. The magisterium noted that there is an intrinsic connection between the act of sexual intercourse and procreation and then proceeded to create a shaky bridge over a theoretical chasm by insisting "that each and every marital act must of necessity retain its intrinsic relationship to the procreation of human life."[18] This insistence represents a strain of natural law thinking, preoccupied with an act-mentality biologism, which is the result of a circumspect deference to Pius XI's *Casti Connubii.* The magisterium did not hesitate to recommend that the value of keeping each and every marital act open to the procreation of human life could be preserved by the practice of the rhythm method.[19] This cast other doubts on what constitutes "natural" in an argument that purports to be based on natural law.

An equally controversial argument against the use of birth control, which has drawn a concentrated and prolonged reaction from ranks within and even outside the Church, was that obedience was due to the document by virtue of the fact that it had been promulgated by the official magisterium, which "enjoy[s] a special light of the Holy Spirit in teaching the truth."[20] The members of the magisterium are "constituted . . . as authentic guardians and interpreters of the whole moral law, not only, that is, of the law of the Gospel but also of the natural law. For the natural law, too, declares the will of God, and its faithful observance is necessary for men's eternal salvation."[21] Basing his command for compliance on the uniqueness of the magisterium's special light and the magisterium's authentic guardianship of the natural law, Paul VI affirmed the unquestionable competence of the hierarchical magisterium: "And this, rather than the arguments they put forward, is why you are bound to such obedience."[22]

The ensuing theological arguments connected the two concerns, making the case in a variety of ways that because of the deficient presentation against the practice of all forms of artificial birth control, the magisterium failed to maintain competence and credibility, which together would constitute a binding authority over the faithful.[23] The effect on the Church has proven to be a lasting one, and many have since asserted that the issuance and subsequent rejection of *Humanae Vitae* have come to represent a watershed in the history of the encyclical tradition in particular and the self-understanding of the Church in general.[24]

Our special concern with regard to *Humanae Vitae* is the third major section of the encyclical, "Pastoral Directives." We ask of this encyclical, and particularly of this section, What is implied by the "pastoral directives" of this moral teaching? The answer to that question may provide clues about an operative but not wholly articulated model of pastoral moral discernment in magisterial teachings. It may also exemplify a broader concern regarding the relationship of "pastoral" to "moral" in official moral teachings and even in the approaches of traditional Catholic moral theology to the interpretation of these teachings.[25] We examine this part of the teaching as an illustration of the problem and lacuna in current Catholic moral theology and practice which we described in the introduction. Our proposal offers the prospect of more adequately enlightening pastoral discernment about moral issues. More broadly, though, this project points toward the renewal of Catholic moral theology itself through an incorporation of the pastoral setting as a vital source for a moral theology in genuine service to the Church.

According to the encyclical, pastoral translation, interpretation, and implementation are matters for properly teaching and uniformly promulgating a legally binding doctrine about the duties of marriage and the prohibitions against birth control. Merciful allowances are then made for those who cannot abide by the teaching. In the thirteen sections (19–31) devoted to the heading "Pastoral Directives," which are addressed generally to the observance of the teaching and specifically to various affected constituencies of its audience, the word "law" or its derivation is mentioned fourteen times, "teaching" or "doctrine" nine times, and some form of "obey" seven times. There are pointed allusions to the "difficulty" and the "burden" that the teaching represents in the lives of married couples, but couples are nonetheless not to "lose heart because of their weakness" in considering those difficulties. Instead, they are to be comforted by scriptural consolations such as "the gate is narrow and the way is hard, that leads to life" and "the form of this world is passing away," and by the spiritual strength of prayer, the Eucharist, and in case "sin still exercises its hold over them," by the sacrament of Penance. Confidence is expressed in the couples that "complete mastery over themselves and their emotions," "self-discipline," "self-denial," and "constan[cy] in their resolution" will triumph over those hardships.

This conception of the pastoral translation of a moral exhortation is witnessed most clearly in Section 28 addressed to priests, the rank-

and-file pastoral ministers, who, "by virtue of [their] sacred office act as counselors and spiritual leaders both of individual men and women and of families." The "principal duty" of these pastors is "to spell out clearly and completely the Church's teaching on marriage" and to inculcate by their own example "sincere obedience, inward as well as outward, which is due to the magisterium of the Church." The priests themselves will possess the requisite confidence in spelling out the teaching: "For, as you know, the pastors of the Church enjoy a special light of the Holy Spirit in teaching the truth." (Whether the word "pastors" in this statement refers to the magisterium or to the priests is unclear, and the ambiguity may be intended.)

In the following section, priests are also buoyed in their confidence that the Holy Spirit "illumines from within the hearts of the faithful and invites their assent." Pastors are connected to the magisterium in a subsidiary way. Indeed, the issue of the unconditional competence of the magisterium takes on added significance when placed in the context of this section on the duties of pastoral ministers: "And this, rather than the arguments they put forward, is why you are bound to such obedience." Perfect obedience by those pastors leads to a univocal pastoral interpretation, a uniformity which serves the people, who take their moral cues from the pastors:

> Nor will it escape you that if men's peace of soul and the unity of the Christian people are to be preserved, then it is of the utmost importance that in moral as well as in dogmatic theology all should obey the magisterium of the Church and should speak as with one voice.

After outlining at length this moral duty of pastors, and noting for good measure that "it is an outstanding manifestation of charity toward souls to omit nothing from the saving doctrine of Christ," the encyclical grants that the teaching in response to magisterial promptings, "must always be joined with tolerance and charity, as Christ Himself showed in His conversations and dealings with men." The recommendation in Section 29, entitled "Christian Compassion," is that the pastor, in imitation of Christ, will not be "bitterly severe toward sin, but patient and abounding in mercy toward sinners."

Revealing perhaps more than was intended, the passage which follows on the heels of this recommendation for mercy toward sinners declares that "husbands and wives, *therefore*, distressed by reason of the difficulties of their life, must find stamped in the heart and voice of their priest the likeness of the voice and the love of our Redeemer." The use of the word "therefore" at this particular juncture discloses a model of pastoral ministry in moral matters that is primarily concerned with the accurate, unmitigated promulgation of teachings and yet includes a compensatory compassion toward *sinners* who cannot live up to the moral exhortations of the magisterium.

In this critical placement of the exercise of compassion on sinners within the pastoral directives about a moral message, compassion assumes the function of the only possible moral solution short of the enactment of the recommended teaching. According to this understanding, the role of the pastor in moral matters is either to act as a conduit for the teaching magisterium or to comfort and then absolve the culpability of those who fail and thus sin in the realization of that teaching.

In relation to the foundational ethic for pastoral moral discernment which we have developed, the underlying ethical framework of *Humanae Vitae* differs significantly. Its framework, moreover, has directly influenced the shape of its "Pastoral Directives." While our foundational ethic, which is based on interactional theories, is grounded in history and the historical method, *Humanae Vitae* embraces a fixed, "classicist" worldview which looks to a biological natural law as the methodological base on which it builds its argument against the practice of birth control. In Section 10, we find that responsible parenthood is not only a matter of attending to "biological laws that apply to the human person," we are told that these laws are part of the "objective moral order that was established by God." Moreover, this natural law for procreative "faculties" is part of the "order of reality established by God" (Section 16).

In addition, this natural law is confluent with the divine moral law, which is promulgated as "the moral doctrine on marriage constantly taught by the magisterium" (Section 6), who are the "authentic guardians and interpreters of the whole moral law" (Section 4). Unlike our foundational ethic, which seeks moral determinations in the interpretations of discrete events and changing human experiences, the fixed moral order of *Humanae Vitae* deduces moral determinations from the compliance to and deviation from the objective moral order, eternally established in the mind and will of the Creator, and unalterably interpreted by the magisterium.

This basic difference in ethical framework influences the model of pastoral moral discernment that flows from it. Discernment, shaped by the foundational ethic that we have forged, places confidence in the experience, growth, development, and influences of and on the agent(s) over time. It tends less toward norms derived from first-order principles and more toward these dynamic factors as indicators for a determination of moral action. The pastoral minister may proceed according to the following maxim: *All determined moral actions occur in a continuum of actions and interactions; these determinations possess meaning in the broader context of a developing personal story.* With specific regard to the practice of the regulation of birth, the minister may pursue the following questions: What is the history of this relationship? How does the familial background of the spouses influence the discussion of the morality of birth regulation? What events and situations have influenced the moral development of the individual spouses and the marriage? What have their principal criteria been for making common moral discernments? What norms or principles do the couple and the minister count as important in considering the practice of birth control? How will this determination culminate in practical action? Is the means of birth control significant? Will the couple maintain an ongoing discussion of the decision between themselves and with others if necessary?

In contrast, the minister who strictly follows the pastoral directives of *Humanae Vitae* would "discern" with a married couple their compliance or noncompliance (and culpability) in regard to a fixed legal paradigm authored by God, taught by the church's magisterium, and transmitted by ministers who answer to the magisterium. Discernment may at best become a "plea bargain" of sorts, whereby exceptions may be made in the name of compassion for sinners who agree to plead to a lesser crime against the objective moral order.

According to our foundational ethic, moral anthropology is multi-dimensional. The human person is an agent who responds to the events of life on numerous levels, including the intellectual and emotional levels. According to this anthropology, the person may have "characteristic" ways of responding, but the actual form of the response is open to change, renewal, and transformation. In *Humanae Vitae*, however, we encounter evidence of a different view of the human person: A decidedly static biologism, borrowed and creatively interpreted from Thomas Aquinas, suggests that the human person is morally determined by "biological laws that apply to the human person" (Section 10). The document also contains a deference to the human will as the focal point of moral determinations. Aligning all actions with the "will of the Author of life" (Section 13), the person is exhorted in numerous places to "resolutely obey," "observe," "strive," and "persevere" in the commands of that will, and "acquire mastery over [them]selves" through self-discipline (Section 21). This sheer willfulness is to be exercised to express a love that is "fully human," and "not merely . . . a question of natural instinct or emotional drive." Not having explained the meaning of the terms "natural instinct" or "emotional drive," the document inculcates a general skepticism about the contributions of dimensions of the human person other than the will, and the "aid of reason" (Section 21) which informs the will.

We can predict the contrasting methods of pastoral moral discernment that will result from these different moral anthropologies. In our relational understanding, the human person is considered in many aspects, including the emotions, the senses and intuitions, the intellectual capacity for reasonable analysis, and the enduring moral traits which have been termed "character." For the purposes of pastoral discernment, the operative maxim is this: Mature moral agency consists of a plurality of personal strengths, including rational understanding and critical distance from the situation, emotional health and sensitivity in the forms of compassion and empathy, and the ability to enact a moral resolution. Pastoral moral discernment about birth control will consciously attend to those aspects in an individual and a couple. Representative questions by the minister may include: What is the couple's understanding of the issue at hand? Why is it an issue at all? Can they appreciate the intellectual integrity of arguments for and against the practice of birth regulation? How do they characterize the emotional health of their relationship, and what effect will children have on it? Will the practice affect the spouses' "character"?[26] What emotional difficulties do they anticipate either in practicing or forgoing birth control? How do they sense God in the creation and sustenance of their own marriage and family? What is the couple's attitude toward the authority of the church in this or other matters? Do they feel bound to follow the teaching on birth regulation? What practical resolutions need to be made so that a moral determination can be realized?

On the other hand, given the moral anthropology of *Humanae Vitae*, pastoral discernment will more likely concern itself with rational arguments to compel the will, based on the consistency of an action in relation to the objective moral commands of natural and

divine law. Aspects of the human person other than will and reason—"emotional drives" and "natural instincts," for example—are
regarded as untrustworthy gauges of moral capacities and therefore
relative distractions in pastoral moral discernment.

Consistent with the affirmation of history and a multivalent moral
anthropology, our foundational ethic allows room for subjective, creative, and inductive judgments of the agent in the course of moral
discernment. Central to this emphasis is the use of subjective images,
vision, and symbols. A premium is placed on "fitting" action that is
practically tailored to the moral demands of the situation. One of the
guiding criteria for such subjective discernment is the question "What
is God enabling and requiring me to do in this situation?" The individual is able to take a reading and make an interpretation in
response to that question. Such considerations may be summarized
as follows: Moral agency entails the capacities to entertain symbolic
interpretive frameworks for discussing an intended action, to imagine
alternative courses of action which correspond to the demands of the
situation, and to envision consequences of various actions. Questions
the minister might profitably pose include: Is there a governing image
in the individual lives of the spouses or the collective life of the couple
by which they see marital love and parenthood? How does the practice of birth regulation fit or fail to fit the image? Do they have a sense
of a symbolic meaning of sexuality, over and against, for example, a
deontological understanding of it? What consequences does the couple envision for alternative courses of action, and can the couple formulate tailored practical responses to the various consequences?

In *Humanae Vitae* there are virtually no allusions to the individual's capacity to read or interpret a situation and subsequently determine a moral action. In one scant reference to a subjective discernment in Section 10 on "Responsible Parenthood," the encyclical
grants that responsible parenthood is exercised by those who,

> With regard to physical, economic, psychological and social con-
> ditions . . . prudently and generously decide to have more chil-
> dren, and by those, who, for serious reason and with due respect
> to moral precepts, decide not to have additional children for
> either a certain or an indefinite period of time.

But true responsible parenthood, the message continues, "has one
further essential aspect of paramount importance," involving the

"objective moral order which was established by God, and of which a right conscience is the true interpreter." So, the argument continues,

> . . . they are not free to act as they choose in the service of transmitting life, as if it were wholly up to them to decide what is the right course to follow. On the contrary, they are bound to insure that what they do corresponds to the will of God the Creator.

The challenge, then, for the pastoral minister in our proposed method of pastoral moral discernment is maieutic; he or she must elicit from the discerner the guiding creative images, symbols, and visions that lead to fitting and responsible moral action. By contrast, the challenge or "principal duty" for the pastoral minister according to the "Pastoral Directives" of *Humanae Vitae* is didactic; he must spell out "clearly and completely the church's teaching on marriage."

The social and relational nature of morality is a central feature of our foundational ethic. Starting with Haan's thesis and complementing it with Macmurray's and Gustafson's contributions, we have asserted that all moral action must be discerned through some form of communally participative dialogue in which God's enablings and requirements may come to be known. Formulated as a pastoral guideline we would say: Moral agents both offer and receive values through discourse. Within this interactive process with another agent or a community, values are appropriated, developed, nuanced, or rejected. For the Christian moral agent, such communal discourse is a means of developing a response to the question, What is God enabling and requiring me to do? Attending to this guideline, the pastoral minister may be concerned with the following questions in a couple's discernment about birth regulation: Has the couple discussed the practice of birth regulation? What is the outcome of that dialogue? What are the present communal attachments of the couple and do they consider them important in the discernment of this issue? Have they had any experience of grace within the context of relationships or in the Christian community? Do the spouses conceive of their own former or intended families as communities? For the purposes of discernment, do they have a conversational partner who is a worthy representative of the Christian tradition as it is articulated, for example, in biblical and magisterial sources?

Virtually no provision is made in *Humanae Vitae* for such an interactional understanding of the moral life. Although as we have seen, the priest acts as "counselor and spiritual leader both of individual men and women and of families," the document quickly identifies such counseling and leading as teaching and further qualifies that role by calling for compassion for sinners.

The difference in the method of pastoral care derived from these ethical understandings is apparent. According to the interactional method, the pastoral minister acts as a participant in an interchange that includes communal truth claims and which has as its term a consensual resolution. The basic stance of the pastoral minister in the view of *Humanae Vitae* is that of an active guardian of doctrine who passes along truth to a passive, inquiring faithful. More is at issue here than the style of communication in pastoral assistance. Woven into *Humanae Vitae*'s description of the role of pastoral minister is a fundamental skepticism that persons in an "equalizing" dialogue can reach a truly moral determination that respects church teaching and the position of the discerning individual or couple.

Finally, our foundational ethic asserts that the moral response of the believing Christian is centered on a relationship to God in Christ by the power of the Holy Spirit, with the dispositions, interpretations of experience, and normative considerations of the believer's moral response shaped by a commitment to "relate all things to their proper relations to God." This God-centered moral response is illuminated and empowered as the believer looks to Jesus Christ as the definitive revelation of God. Succinctly stated for pastoral purposes: The Christian moral agent appropriates meaning by incorporating his or her story in the broader message of the Christian narrative. Lest the couple's discernment regarding birth control be conducted outside of the realm of particular and personal faith, the minister may inquire along the following lines: Can the spouses articulate this and other moral turning points as a continuation of the story of Jesus and the ensuing Christian tradition? Do they have any personal experience of transformation or empowerment through the healing and forgiveness revealed by God in Christ? How do they see their own intended family life as a Christian vocation or form of discipleship?

By contrast, if the basic thrust of *Humanae Vitae* may be termed an effort to "relate things to their proper relations to God," the effort is to relate all things to the immutable moral law of God, uniquely interpreted and promulgated by the magisterium, in keeping with the truth that

> Jesus Christ, when He communicated His divine power to Peter and the other Apostles and sent them to teach all nations His commandments, constituted them as the authentic guardians and interpreters of the whole moral law, not only, that is, of the law of the Gospel but also of the natural law.[27]

Again we see the pervasive presence of the legal and pedagogical paradigm. One's relationship to God is equated with one's relationship to God's law, and the role of Jesus Christ as the definitive revelation of God is narrowed to the role of Jesus' teaching authority in bearing that revelation.

In our proposed method of pastoral moral discernment, the charge to make all discernment God-centered through Jesus Christ by the power of the Holy Spirit includes the forming and transforming of the dispositions, the experience and normative considerations of the moral agent through a variety of scriptural sources and genres, as well as the Christian tradition articulated as official magisterial teachings, but also communal worship and wisdom. From the interactional perspective, the God-centered formation and transformation of the agent is effected in a number of different ways by diverse means. By contrast, *Humanae Vitae* suggests a pastoral moral discernment that is restricted to scriptural sources and genres favoring the commands of God and their authoritative promulgation by Jesus, and to church tradition characterized as official, legal, customary, and instructional.

This contrast completes our formulation of an interactional pastoral practice. By developing a foundational ethic and a critical method for pastoral moral discernment grounded in an interactional perspective, we are ultimately suggesting a new direction for Roman Catholic pastoral practice. Certainly more can be done to refine this suggestion for pastoral implementation. Beyond that call for further study and proposition, the interactional foundational ethic and its practical implementation in the pastoral setting can imply a new direction for Catholic moral theology. With due respect for the contributions of the interactional perspective as it is articulated in moral psychology, philosophy, and theology, Catholic moral theology may discover a rich source for formulating a theology of moral experience that is both respectful of a relational understanding of the human person and faithful to God in Christ.

NOTES

1. For an extensive treatment of the role of norms and principles in Christian ethics, see Gene Outka and Paul Ramsey, *Norm and Context in Christian Ethics* (New York: Charles Scribner's Sons, 1968). Also see Richard Gula, *What Are They Saying About Moral Norms* (Ramsey: Paulist Press, 1982), especially Chapter 5, "Moral Norms and Pastoral Guidance."

2. For a discussion of the proper relationship of norms to discernment of a particular course of action, see Timothy E. O'Connell, *Principles for a Catholic Morality* (Minneapolis: Seabury Press, 1978), Chapter 15, "Morality: Values and Norms," especially pp. 163–164.

3. For an interesting dialogue between psychological theories of moral development and Christian belief, see Bonnidell Clouse, *Moral Development: Perspectives in Psychology and Christian Belief* (Grand Rapids, MI: Baker Book House, 1985).

4. On the balance between empathic and moral considerations in pastoral counseling, see Don S. Browning, *The Moral Context of Pastoral Care* (Philadelphia: Westminster Press, 1976), Chapter Five, "Toward a Model of Care," especially, p. 106.

5. Browning recognizes the role of intuitive experience in moral decision making, but assigns it a complementary role in his five-level model of practical moral thinking. See *Religious Ethics and Pastoral Care* (Philadelphia: Fortress Press, 1983), Chapter Five.

6. Gustafson, *Can Ethics Be Christian?*, 47.

7. The most widely recognized spokesperson for the notion of Christian character and its relation to Christian tradition and narrative is Stanley Hauerwas. See, for example, *Character and the Christian Life* (San Antonio: Trinity University Press, 1975); *Vision and Virtue* (Notre Dame: Fides Publishers, 1975); *Truthfulness and Tragedy* (with Richard Bondi and David Burrell) (Notre Dame: University of Notre Dame Press, 1977); *A Community of Character* (Notre Dame: University of Notre Dame Press, 1981).

8. For a classical formulation of the role of imagination in discernment, see Nos. 179–188, *The Spiritual Exercises of St. Ignatius*, trans. Louis J. Puhl, S.J. (Chicago: Loyola University Press. First printing: Newman Press, 1951).

9. Recent contributions to this discussion of the relationship between imagination and Christian ethics include Philip S. Keane, *Christian Ethics and Imagination* (Ramsey: Paulist Press, 1984) and Craig Dykstra, *Vision and Character: A Christian Educator's Alternative To Kohlberg* (Ramsey: Paulist Press, 1981).

10. Haan, et al., *On Moral Grounds*, 48–49, 51.

11. Ibid., 50.

12.   The legitimate inclusion of self-interests in moral discernment is especially germane to the emerging role of women in many cultures. Carol Gilligan's call for more integrated moral vision between the genders entails men taking more seriously the perspective and ideal of relationality and women developing a sense of autonomy. It seems that for Gilligan, what is at stake for women is precisely this issue of subverting the legitimate self-interests of women in creating a cultural "common good." See the last chapter of *In a Different Voice.*

13.   H. Richard Niebuhr, *The Responsible Self* (Harper and Row, New York: 1978), see Chapter One, "The Meaning of Responsibility," especially pp. 60 ff.

See also William C. Spohn, "The Ethics of the Fitting: H. Richard Niebuhr and the American Tradition," an essay delivered September 9, 1988, at a conference at Harvard University celebrating the twenty-fifth anniversary of Niebuhr's death. Spohn discusses other appropriations of the ethics of the "fitting" by three authors in the American speculative tradition, Jonathan Edwards, William James, and John Dewey, and how one might draw from them a fuller appreciation of Niebuhr's notion.

14.   With the formulation of "The Challenge to Peace" and "Economic Justice for All," for example, the United States Bishops have demonstrated that such a method would not be wholly impracticable. The interactional offering and reception of expert and experiential testimony in the formulation of the two teachings, roundly commended as a method in both scholarly and non-scholarly circles, increased credibility and publicity for the documents.

15.   Gustafson, *The Church as Moral Decision-Maker*, 130–131. It is interesting to note that this skepticism about the far-reaching expertise of the pastor is specifically mentioned in Vatican II's Pastoral Constitution on the Church in the Modern World, *Gaudium et Spes*, No. 43, "The Help Which the Church Strives to Give to Human Activity Through Christians": "From priests [the laity] may look for spiritual light and nourishment. Let the layman not imagine that his pastors are always such experts, that to every problem that arises, however complicated, they can readily give him a concrete solution, or even that such is their mission. Rather, enlightened by Christian wisdom and giving close attention to the teaching authority of the Church, let the layman take on his own distinctive role."

16.   With due respect to Gustafson, from whom we draw the basic assertion that Christ illuminates and empowers a moral response on the part of the believer, Gustafson himself seems at best tentative about what "empowers" might mean. We noted in Chapter 4 that as is especially evidenced in his later work, Gustafson holds a relatively "low" christology, so that beyond the empowerment which comes from the inspiration of Christ's message, we meet carefully crafted silence from Gustafson about an entitative change in the believer by virtue of Christ's ongoing saving action by the power of the Holy Spirit. Niebuhr has the same basic scheme of an ethics of responsibility and fitting action but has the believing agent responding to "the One who heals all our diseases, forgives all our iniquities, saves our lives from destruction, and crowns us with everlasting mercy" (H. Richard Niebuhr, *The Responsible Self*, 144–145).

17. Valuable resources in this regard are Charles E. Curran and Richard A. McCormick, eds., *Readings in Moral Theology IV: The Use of Scripture in Moral Theology* (Ramsey: Paulist Press, 1984); William C. Spohn, *What Are They Saying About Scripture and Ethics?* (Ramsey: Paulist Press, 1984); Kenneth R. Himes, "Scripture and Ethics: A Review Essay," *Biblical Theology Bulletin* 15 (April 1985): 65–73; and James M. Gustafson, "The Place of Scripture in Christian Ethics: A Methodological Study," *Theology and Christian Ethics* (Philadelphia: United Church Press), 121–145.

18. Paul VI, *Humanae Vitae*, Section 11, in Claudia Carlen, I.H.M., *The Papal Encyclicals 1958–1981* (New York: McGrath Publishing, 1981), 226.

19. Ibid., Section 16, 227.

20. Ibid., Section 28, 231.

21. Ibid., Section 4, 224.

22. Ibid., Section 28, 231.

23. A typically masterful review of theological reflection on *Humanae Vitae* is done by Richard McCormick in *Notes on Moral Theology 1965–1980* (Lanham, MD: University Press of America, 1981), 233–266, and *Notes on Moral Theology 1980–1984* (Lanham, MD: University Press of America, 1984).

24. Albert R. Jonsen and Stephen Toulmin suggest that *Humanae Vitae* represents the beginning of the decline of the "centralization of the authority in the moral sphere." See *The Abuse of Casuistry: A History of Moral Reasoning* (Berkeley: University of California Press, 1988), 271.

25. Richard McCormick, S.J., has helpfully pointed out that much of my discussion illuminating the pastoral approach of *Humanae Vitae* is secondary to the issue of whether the argument of the encyclical is adequate. That is, perhaps the best approach to pastoral moral discernment about artificial birth control would be to address the argument and not merely the pastoral directives of *Humanae Vitae*. Nonetheless, the "Pastoral Directives" of *Humanae Vitae* illustrate well the suggested connection between the moral directives of official Church teachings and role of pastors in promulgating and interpreting those teachings.

26. For an excellent treatment of the connection between "character" and the procreative ethics of *Humanae Vitae*, see Jeremiah J. McCarthy, "A Discernment Model for the Ethics of Birth Control: An Application of a Narrative Method With Critical Observations," Ph.D. dissertation, Graduate Theological Union, 1985.

27. Paul VI, *Humanae Vitae*, Section 4, 224.